JAMES CITY:

A BLACK COMMUNITY
IN NORTH CAROLINA
1863-1900

JAMES CITY:
A BLACK COMMUNITY IN NORTH CAROLINA 1863-1900

By Joe A. Mobley

*Research Reports from the
Division of Archives and History*

Number 1

Raleigh
North Carolina Department of Cultural Resources
Division of Archives and History
1981

Publication of this volume was subsidized by a grant from the May Gordon
Latham Kellenberger Historical Foundation.

DEPARTMENT OF CULTURAL RESOURCES

Sara W. Hodgkins
Secretary

DIVISION OF ARCHIVES AND HISTORY

William S. Price, Jr.
Director

Suellen M. Hoy
Assistant Director

NORTH CAROLINA HISTORICAL COMMISSION

Mrs. Frank A. Daniels, Jr.
Chairman

T. Harry Gatton
Vice-Chairman

CONTENTS

ILLUSTRATIONS

FOREWORD

For many years members of the staffs of the Historic Sites and Archaeology and Historic Preservation sections of the Division of Archives and History have done research and written reports of their findings for use in the work of the programs of those two sections. Used almost exclusively for internal projects, the reports have had limited readership outside the division. Some of the research was of such significance that a wider use of the reports seemed advisable, and in the fall of 1980 plans were announced for publication of the report or reports completed between July 1, 1979, and June 30, 1980, deemed most worthy by the Advisory Editorial Committee of the *North Carolina Historical Review*. Four reports were submitted. Because of their length, it was determined that only one could be published, and the one selected by the committee was *James City: A Black Community in North Carolina, 1863-1900*, by Joe A. Mobley, a member of the staff of the Research Branch, Archaeology and Historic Preservation Section.

Abstracts of all research reports were submitted with the full studies. Two of those abstracts appear on pages 111 and 113 of this publication following Mr. Mobley's report; the third was withdrawn by its author. All of the full reports are available in the offices of the sections in which they were produced and may be consulted by any interested researcher.

The Division of Archives and History, in announcing plans for this first study, projected an annual publication. It is hoped that future reports will be of quality to merit publication and that appropriations for printing will be sufficient to support this plan. The Division of Archives and History is grateful to the May Gordon Latham Kellenberger Historical Foundation of New Bern for making possible the publication of this first report. The foundation was supportive of the James City study because of the black community's Craven County location. Without the Kellenberger grant, this publication could not have been issued.

James City: A Black Community was edited by Robert M. Topkins, historical publications editor in the Historical Publications Section. In seeing the report through the press, he was assisted by Patricia R. Johnson, proofreader in the section.

MEMORY F. MITCHELL
Historical Publications Administrator

June 18, 1981

ACKNOWLEDGMENTS

The author wishes to express his gratitude to several persons who contributed time and effort to help ensure the completion of this study. He is indebted to Dr. Jerry C. Cashion, Dr. William C. Harris, and Marie D. Moore for reading the draft and making suggestions. Gratitude is also due Prisca Crettier for typing the manuscript. The people of James City, especially James C. Delemar and Isaac Long, deserve a special note of thanks for their patience and kind assistance.

INTRODUCTION

The black community of James City is located just across the Trent River from New Bern in Craven County. Many of the people who presently reside there are descendants of former slaves who populated the area during the Civil War and Reconstruction.

The story of the black village begins with the seizure of New Bern by the Union army in March, 1862. Following its capture and subsequent occupation, New Bern became a refugee center for thousands of North Carolina slaves who sought freedom and safety within Union lines. In an effort to accommodate the escaped blacks, United States Army chaplain Horace James in 1863 established a camp for freedmen near New Bern. At first the camp was known as the Trent River settlement or Trent River camp; but toward the close of the war it came to be called James City in honor of its founder, who was then an officer of the Freedmen's Bureau. James had a significant impact upon the settlement, and his career in North Carolina is part of the James City narrative.

From the immediate postwar period until about 1900, James City remained a cohesive black community whose inhabitants struggled collectively to secure an economic and political foothold. James City blacks were economically productive, politically active, and eager to be educated; their primary goal throughout this period was to obtain permanent ownership of the land on which they resided as tenants. To achieve that end, they fought a long but unsuccessful court battle. When they failed to win their case in 1893, their community began to dissolve. During the late nineteenth and early twentieth centuries, residents began to depart the settlement for areas outside the county and state. Others chose to make their homes in the present-day community of James City, which is only a short distance south of the original camp.

In recent years historians have exhibited an intense interest in the history of black Americans and have produced a sizable body of scholarship treating this subject. Most of this scholarship, however, has dealt with the history of blacks on a regional or national level; little attention has been directed toward the study of specific black communities. Because James City remained a stronghold of black self-determination from 1863 to 1900, it affords a useful model for the study of Afro-American history on the local level.

I. NEW BERN BECOMES A MECCA FOR FREEDOM

In March, 1862, many of the slaves in eastern North Carolina anticipated that a great change was about to occur in their lives. Rumors had reached them from Roanoke Island that Yankee soldiers were coming to set them free. Union forces under General Ambrose E. Burnside had indeed landed at Roanoke Island only a month before and were then en route to New Bern.[1] In the spring of 1862 black refugees who came into the Federal lines in North Carolina did not yet enjoy the legal status of freemen, but it was the policy of many Union commanders, including General Burnside, to provide refuge for blacks who fled to territory held by the Union army and to use many of them as laborers.

Although the Emancipation Proclamation was still months in the future, a policy of treating escaped slaves as freemen had already been effected by the Union army. At Fortress Monroe, Virginia, in 1861, Major General Benjamin F. Butler had established the precedent of protecting runaway slaves when he designated some of them as "contraband of war" and refused to return them to their masters. Instead, he utilized them as laborers to assist his army. He assigned to them the name "contrabands," which for a time would apply both to slaves captured by Union forces and as a slang word to refer to Negroes generally. As the war continued, additional United States officers in the South began safeguarding the freedom of fugitive slaves and utilizing their labor. Some did this as a war measure to aid the Union effort, others because they felt that human bondage was morally wrong. Many Federal commanders were motivated by both rationales.[2]

When, after a brief battle with Confederate defenders, the Federals seized New Bern on March 14, the slaves in the area turned out to greet their liberators with shouts of jubilation. William P. Derby, a member of the Twenty-seventh Massachusetts Regiment, recalled that as his unit "landed at the New Berne wharf a darky woman, whose white hair betoken great age," came dancing toward him and grasped him by the arms, exclaiming, "Bress the Lord, Massa! I ze bein prain fur uze dese forty years! I taut uze nebber coming tall! but uze come at las! Bress the

---

[1] For an account of Burnside's expedition to Roanoke Island and the battle for New Bern, see John G. Barrett, *The Civil War in North Carolina* (Chapel Hill: University of North Carolina Press, 1963), 95-113, hereinafter cited as Barrett, *Civil War in North Carolina*.

[2] J. G. Randall and David Donald, *The Civil War and Reconstruction* (Lexington, Mass.: D. C. Heath and Company, second edition, enlarged, 1969), 371, hereinafter cited as Randall and Donald, *Civil War and Reconstruction*; Leon F. Litwack, *Been in the Storm So Long: The Aftermath of Slavery* (New York: Alfred A. Knopf, 1979), 52, hereinafter cited as Litwack, *Been in the Storm So Long*.

Lord!" "Her features," Derby later wrote, "were suffused with joy during the effervescence, and the loose planks of the wharf kept time with her dance and gesticulations. [Hers] was a simple faith which recognized the providence of God in the fruition of a long-deferred hope." Shortly thereafter, Derby witnessed a similar expression of black elation:

A [white] man [he wrote] was evidently making the best of the last opportunity to escape, and was well out beyond where our fortifications were afterwards placed, when a shell thrown over the city by our guns, buried itself in the ground and exploded just behind him, covering him with dust and dirt. A darkey near us who had been intently watching him, exclaimed, "Judy see dar! Dars Massa running awa, an de vengence of de Lord is arter him."[3]

As word spread that the Union liberators had occupied New Bern, large numbers of slaves left nearby farms and plantations and came to the city to seek their freedom. For many, freedom was as close as the Union lines, sometimes only down a road or across a river. They left the homes of their masters, hid in the woods or swamps during the day, and then made their way to the Federal troops, usually at New Bern but also at Washington, Elizabeth City, or other points held by the United States Army. Hattie Rogers, an Onslow County slave, described the flight that some blacks made to escape bondage. "When the Yankees took New Bern," she later recalled, "all who could swim the [White Oak] river and get to the Yankees were free. Some of the men swum the river and got to Jones County then to New Bern and freedom."[4]

When Union troops departed New Bern on forays into the interior near Goldsboro, Kinston, Tarboro, or some other place, many slaves left their homes and joined the soldiers on their return to New Bern. Corporal James A. Emmerton of the Twenty-third Massachusetts Regiment, which was stationed in New Bern, remembered that "every expedition to the interior . . . was a sign for great numbers to come in."[5] In August, 1862, a Confederate officer estimated the monetary value of fleeing slaves to be $1 million per week.[6]

---

[3] W. P. Derby, Bearing Arms in the Twenty-seventh Massachusetts Regiment of Volunteer Infantry during the Civil War, 1861-1865 (Boston: Wright and Potter Printing Company, 1883), 94-95.

[4] George P. Rawick (ed.), The American Slave: A Composite Autobiography (Westport, Conn.: Greenwood Press, 19 volumes, 1972-1977), Volume 14: North Carolina Narratives, Part II, 227-228, hereinafter cited as Rawick, The American Slave . . . North Carolina Narratives.

[5] James A. Emmerton, A Record of the Twenty-third Regiment Mass. Vol. Infantry in the War of the Rebellion, 1861-1865 . . . (Boston: William Ware and Company, 1886), 95, hereinafter cited as Emmerton, Record of the Twenty-third Regiment.

[6] Litwack, Been in the Storm So Long, 52.

Federal troops landing near New Bern, March, 1862. Engraving from Alfred H. Guernsey and Henry M. Alden, *Harper's Pictorial History of the Civil War* (Chicago: Star Publishing Company, 2 volumes, 1894), I, p. 246.

Most of these slaves had no comprehension of what the future held in store for them. "Possessed of the single idea of personal freedom," noted Emmerton, "they took no thought of how they were to be supported. Some of them seemed to have no idea that the change meant anything but a new, and, they hoped, a kinder master." Emmerton recalled that on one occasion "a young mother brought a cartload of her black pickaninnies to the lines, and when asked to whom the horse and vehicle belonged had no answer but 'to you all massa.'"[7]

Although slaves may not always have been certain of what freedom entailed, they were certain that it had to be a change for the better. As in other southern states, the conditions of slavery in North Carolina varied according to masters. Some owners were brutal and abused their slaves. Others were kinder and were accorded a degree of loyalty by servants such as Henry Roundtree, who testified that "ole marster doan live long atter de war am over but till de day he was buried we all done anything he ax us." But whether their masters were kind or cruel men, most slaves longed for freedom and took any clear opportunity to gain it. Perhaps North Carolina slave Tom Wilcox best conveyed the prevalent desire among blacks to control their own destiny:

De white folks wuz good ter us an' we loved 'em but we wanted to be free, case de Lawd done make us all free. . . . We wuz fed an' clothed good an' we lived for each other, but my pappy belonged ter one man an' my mammy to another an' so we wanted to be all together.[8]

---

[7] Emmerton, *Record of the Twenty-third Regiment*, 95.
[8] Rawick, *The American Slave . . . North Carolina Narratives*, Part II, 235, 377-378.

3

Former slaves knew that the actions of Union soldiers were responsible for their new status as freemen. Corporal Z. T. Haines of the Forty-fourth Massachusetts Regiment, who traveled from Morehead City to New Bern by rail in October, 1862, observed the pleasure with which slaves consistently greeted newly arriving Federal troops:

> Occasional negro villages and scattered negro huts were objects of lively interest. All hands turned out to see us as we shot past. The men showed their entire ivory and the women threw their black arms up and down in the most vehement approbation.
> At dusk we crossed the river Neuse, and found ourselves in the pretty little city of New Bern, where, as may be guessed, we received a hearty welcome from the Massachusetts men stationed [there]. Our friends the contrabands were not the least enthusiastic of those who welcomed us.[9]

In the second year of the Civil War the action taken by Union commanders to guarantee the liberty of contrabands was given further sanction by officials in Washington, D.C. President Abraham Lincoln declared in June, 1862, that "no slave who once comes within our lines as fugitive from a rebel, shall ever be returned to his master."[10] Congress on June 17, 1862, likewise passed a confiscation act that declared all slaves who were the property of persons engaged in treason against the United States to be freemen. These edicts did not, however, apply to those slave owners who were still loyal to the United States. It remained for the Emancipation Proclamation, first issued as a preliminary document in September, 1862, and promulgated in its final form in January, 1863, to liberate all slaves within states then in rebellion against the United States.[11]

As North Carolina slaves poured into New Bern, General Burnside, like other Union commanders in the South, faced the problem of how to care for and employ the ever growing number of black fugitives. He was also saddled with the problem of providing aid for many native whites who had been made destitute by the war. To meet these problems Burnside appointed Vincent Colyer as superintendent of the poor for the Federally occupied areas of North Carolina. Before the war Colyer had been a resident of Washington, D.C., where he had worked as an

---

[9] "Corporal" [Z. T. Haines], Letters from the Forty-fourth Regiment M.V.M. [Massachusetts Volunteer Militia]: A Record of the Experience of a Nine Months' Regiment in the Department of North Carolina in 1862-3 (Boston: Herald Job Office, 1863), 35, hereinafter cited as "Corporal," Letters from the Forty-fourth Regiment M.V.M.

[10] Vincent Colyer, Report of the Services Rendered by the Freed People to the United States Army, in North Carolina, in the Spring of 1862, After the Battle of Newbern (New York: Vincent Colyer, 1864), 51, hereinafter cited as Colyer, Report of the Services Rendered by the Freed People.

[11] Randall and Donald, Civil War and Reconstruction, 372-373.

4

New Bern harbor as it appeared ca. 1862. At right is the Neuse River, at left the Trent River. On the opposite side of the Trent (extreme left) is the future site of the Trent River settlement. Engraving from L. C. Vass, *History of the Presbyterian Church in New Bern, N.C. . . .* (Richmond, Va.: Whittet & Shepperson, 1886), frontispiece.

agent of the New York YMCA. He had worked briefly with the contrabands on Roanoke Island before beginning his duties at his New Bern headquarters on March 30, 1862.[12]

Colyer's first action was to take a census of the people entrusted to his supervision. He enumerated the contrabands in New Bern and its vicinity at 7,500 and counted 10,000 black men, women, and children in the entire Department of North Carolina, which consisted mainly of the coastal area of the state. The largest centers for black refugees were at New Bern, Roanoke Island, Washington, and Beaufort.[13]

The number of slaves seeking refuge in New Bern grew significantly as Federal soldiers came in contact with slaves in the interior. Word spread by way of the slave grapevine that the Yankee soldiers had arrived and liberty was at hand. "There is perhaps not a slave in North Carolina who does not know he can find freedom in New Bern, and thus New Bern may be Mecca of a thousand noble aspirations," declared one Union soldier.[14] Colyer described the arrival of the runaways in New Bern:

The freed people came into my yard from the neighboring plantations, sometimes as many as one hundred at a time, leaving with joy their plows in the fields, and their old homes, to follow our soldiers when returning from their frequent raids; the women carrying their pickannies and the men huge bundles of bedding and clothing occasionally with a cart or old wagon, with a mule drawing their household stuff.

---

[12] Colyer, *Report of the Services Rendered by the Freed People*, 6; Norman D. Brown, *Edward Stanly: Whiggery's Tarheel "Conquerer"* (University, Ala.: University of Alabama Press, 1974), 207, hereinafter cited as Brown, *Edward Stanly*.

[13] Colyer, *Report of the Services Rendered by the Freed People*, 6, 9.

[14] Emmerton, *Record of the Twenty-third Regiment*, 95.

In this view of the headquarters of Vincent Colyer, superintendent of the poor for the Federally occupied areas of North Carolina, the clothing of captured Confederate soldiers is being distributed to local contrabands. Engraving, based on a sketch by J. H. Schell, from *The American Soldier in the Civil War* (New York: Bryan, Taylor & Co., 1895), p. 78.

Having received the fugitives, Colyer and his assistants gave them food, registered their names, and after allowing them a night's sleep found them places to live, frequently in the numerous shanties that were springing up behind Union lines.[15]

Many of these refugees were like George Harris, a Jones County slave whose master at the outbreak of the war told him "dat he expected we would all soon be free." Harris later recalled his flight: "We lived near Trenton. When de Yankees took New Bern, our master had us out in de woods in Jones County mindin hosses an' takin' care o' things he had hid there. We got afraid and ran away to New Bern in Craven County. We all went in a gang and walked. De Yankees took us at Deep Gully ten miles dis side o' New Bern an' carried us inside de lines." The Federals employed Harris's father as a cook and gave various yard and stable jobs to the other men.[16]

General Burnside ordered Colyer to employ up to 5,000 of the fugitive blacks to build fortifications at New Bern and other coastal points in Union hands. The general also instructed him to pay the laborers $8.00 a month and provide them with one ration a day and sufficient clothes.

---

[15] Colyer, *Report of the Services Rendered by the Freed People*, 33, 41.
[16] Rawick, *The American Slave . . . North Carolina Narratives*, Part I, 374.

Vincent Colyer was authorized to employ up to 5,000 former slaves to assist the Federal military effort by constructing fortifications at New Bern and at other points along the North Carolina coast. Engraving from Vincent Colyer, *Report of the Services Rendered by the Freed People* . . . (New York: Vincent Colyer, 1864), p. 7.

During Colyer's tour of duty the contrabands under his care constructed Fort Totten at New Bern, which later played an important role in repelling two attempts by Confederate forces to retake New Bern. Contrabands also built forts on Roanoke Island and at Washington, North Carolina, under Colyer's supervision.[17]

In addition to building fortifications, the former bondsmen in New Bern performed many other essential and difficult tasks in assisting the Union army. They undertook these tasks willingly in order to strike a blow for their liberators and against their former masters. "They considered it duty," Colyer claimed, "and though they could in many cases, have made more money, at other occupations, there was a public opinion among them that tabooed anyone that refused to work for the government." Refugee blacks loaded and unloaded cargoes for about 300 steamers that brought war supplies and served as permanent labor gangs in the quartermaster's commissary and ordnance offices. The former slaves constructed a large railroad bridge across the Trent River (in March, 1862, Confederates had destroyed an earlier bridge) and also built bridges across Batchelor's and other creeks near New Bern as well as docks at Roanoke Island and elsewhere. These construction projects were important to the movement of Union troops and supplies.

The most spectacular and dangerous service performed by the contrabands in New Bern was that of Union spy. The former slaves frequently

---

[17] Colyer, *Report of the Services Rendered by the Freed People*, 6, 9.

New Bern freedmen also assisted the Union army by constructing and repairing railroads (top left), gathering firewood and cooking for army hospitals (top right), and caring for wounded soldiers on the battlefield (bottom). Engravings from Colyer, *Report of the Services Rendered by the Freed People*, pp. 49, 42, and 61 respectively.

traveled from 30 to 300 miles behind Confederate lines to secure information concerning important posts and positions. Union officers praised their service and were impressed by their devotion to duty in the face of danger. Vincent Colyer marveled at the fact that

They visited within the Rebel lines, Kinston, Goldsboro, Trenton, Onslow, Swansboro, Tarboro, and points on the Roanoke River: often on these errands barely escaping with their lives. They were pursued on several occasions by bloodhounds, two or three of them were taken prisoners; one of these was known to have been shot, and the fate of the others was not ascertained. The pay they received for this work was small but satisfactory. They seemed to think their lives were well spent, if necessary, in giving rest, security and success to the

Union troops, whom they regarded as their deliverers. They usually knelt in solemn prayer before they left, and on their return from these hazardous errands, as they considered the work as religious duty.

In 1862 about fifty slave volunteers were kept constantly employed as spies, scouts, and guides for the army.[18]

A number of former slaves contributed to the Union cause by engaging in the "spectacular and dangerous service" of spying on Confederate forces. Shown at left is a typical "Union scout"; at right are scouts engaged in a spying expedition. Engravings from Colyer, *Report of the Services Rendered by the Freed People*, pp. 27 and 28 respectively.

The displaced former slaves usually came to the Union lines (from the interior) with little means of furnishing the necessities of life, but their demands on the federal government were not large. Colyer noted that although there were four times as many fugitive slaves in New Bern as there were destitute whites, he gave sixteen times as many provisions to the whites. Nevertheless, Colyer and the army made significant contributions to the welfare of the blacks in New Bern. When, for example, smallpox appeared in the town, he had the freedmen there vaccinated and induced General Burnside to establish under government supervision a hospital for blacks.

Colyer also established churches for blacks "at no cost to the government."[19] The former bondsmen regarded religion as an important part of their lives, having often turned to it for comfort while in slavery.

---

[18] Colyer, *Report of the Services Rendered by the Freed People*, 9-10.
[19] Colyer, *Report of the Services Rendered by the Freed People*, 31.

Union soldiers witnessed their devotion to worship. Wrote Corporal Z. T. Haines:

Our nights are rendered musical by the plaintive choral hymns of devotional negroes in every direction, alone and in groups. From their open cabins comes the mingled noises of men wrestling painfully and agonizingly with the spirit, and those uttering the ecstatic notes of the redeemed.[20]

Soon after his arrival in New Bern, Colyer preached a service for blacks at their request in the African Methodist church and reopened a black Baptist church that had been closed earlier by whites. Religious meetings were usually crowded. "Without the ability to read, except in a very few instances," Colyer observed, "with but little leisure to attend places of public worship, and through long and painful years of oppression they have been blessed by the grace of God, with a simplicity and clearness of understanding of the fundamental doctrines of the truth of salvation as it is in Jesus Christ, that is most astonishing." Blacks in New Bern founded the first African Methodist Episcopal Zion church in the South. In April, 1864, the black congregation of Andrew Methodist Episcopal Chapel joined the African Methodist Episcopal Zion Conference and renamed their church St. Peter's. They were led in this change by the Reverend (later Bishop) James Walker Hood, who was sent to New Bern by A.M.E. Zion officials in New England in response to a request by the Andrew Chapel congregation. Hood remained for a time as pastor of St. Peter's and subsequently became one of the state's most active and influential black men.

Related in the minds of northerners like Colyer to the religious needs of blacks was the necessity for educating the former slaves. Colyer early established schools for the contrabands and poor whites in New Bern. He engaged a young woman, a resident of the city, to teach the poor whites. For the blacks he began two evening schools with a total of 800 pupils, young and old. Some of the soldiers in the New England regiments, particularly the Twenty-fifth Massachusetts, a number of whom were college graduates, volunteered as teachers.[21]

Blacks placed great value on such education, as soldier-teachers testified. Corporal Emmerton discerned among sawmill workers at New Bern a strong desire to learn. According to Emmerton, each of the workmen had "his spelling book which was speedily whipped out and

---

[20] "Corporal," *Letters from the Forty-fourth Regiment M.V.M.*, 107.
[21] Colyer, *Report of the Services Rendered by the Freed People*, 35-36, 39, 43-44; William J. Walls, *The African Methodist Episcopal Church: Reality of the Black Church* (Charlotte: A.M.E. Zion Publishing House, 1974), 186-189.

10

Superintendent Colyer, aware of the necessity of educating former slaves, in
April, 1862, established a public school for
the contrabands and poor whites in the
vicinity of New Bern. Engraving from
Colyer, *Report of the Services Rendered by
the Freed People*, p. 45.

zealously studied at every break, however short, in their onerous task."
He also reported that the ages of students in the black schools ranged
from 10 to 50 and that, although the capacity of the students to learn
"was as various as their ages, . . . all were eager." On some occasions,
Emmerton recalled, "they were waiting for school to open one and two
hours before the appointed time."[22]

Many of the Union soldiers, such as those who volunteered to be
teachers, were genuinely sympathetic to the blacks who fled to New
Bern. They felt that part of their mission as men-at-arms was to attack
the perpetrators of the immoral institution of slavery. A number of the
young men in the Massachusetts regiments were well educated and
idealistic, and some of them had received theological training and exposure to New England abolitionist dogma. One soldier, George F.
Winston, noted that in his Massachusetts company there were seven-
teen young men from Harvard College, "two of whom were at
theological school at Andover when they enlisted." Also in the company
were about twenty men "from a Christian association in Boston."[23]

But not all of the northern troops were favorably disposed toward the
contrabands. Some frequently resented the men of color and at times
ridiculed or mistreated them. Corporal Z. T. Haines recorded a number

---

[22] Emmerton, *Record of the Twenty-third Regiment*, 96-97.
[23] George F. Winston to a friend or neighbor, February 15, 1863, New Bern Occupation
Papers, Southern Historical Collection, University of North Carolina Library, Chapel
Hill, hereinafter cited as New Bern Occupation Papers.

of instances in which members of his volunteer regiment abused former slaves with cruel jokes and humiliating treatment. He also observed that the "old regiments" would allow no "cullured person' to wear Uncle Sam's buttons, [and] the soldier who returns the salute of a negro is set down as a transgressor of military etiquette." Not a few of the soldiers detested the presence in New Bern of so many of whom they considered an inferior race. "There is nothing but niggers and soldiers in New Bern," remarked one disgruntled member of the Forty-fourth Massachusetts Volunteers.[24] Others resented the attempts by blacks to assert themselves as freemen entitled to pay and privileges for their labor. Union soldier Thomas J. Jennings, for example, wrote home to Fall River, Massachusetts:

You who are home are as ignorant of the position and the qualifications of the Negroes, as they are of education. You ask why we don't make them do the labor; We have been trying to, but it is not a week since that more than 200 were taken under a strong guard to the guard house for refusing duty under the plea that they hadn't been paid. What would you say if the whole army mutinied upon the same plea? And yet some of the troops haven't been paid for 8 months.[25]

Some soldiers bitterly blamed the slaves for the war. Blount Baker, a Wilson County slave, remembered an encounter with Federal soldiers who harbored such resentment: "Dey talk mean to us an' one of dem say dat we niggers am de cause of de war. Sir I sez, 'folks what am a wantin' a war can always find a cause'! He kicks me in de seat of de pants for dat, so I hushes."[26] According to George F. Winston, volunteer troops were the best behaved and the most sympathetic to the blacks. Draftees, he felt, were less disciplined, poorly behaved, and the most likely to provoke trouble with the former slaves.

Despite injustices, the freedmen continued for the most part to view the men in blue as liberators and performed many volunteer tasks for them. Slaves who accompanied the returning expeditions from the interior rendered service to their deliverers by "toting the arms and equipment of tired and lazy soldiers." Blacks in New Bern also bestowed small gifts and treats on the warriors who had freed them. "Gingerbread, pies, and even apple-dumplings are brought to us by the negroes in profusion," wrote one infantryman.[27]

[24] "Corporal," Letters from the Forty-fourth Regiment M.V.M., 37.
[25] Thomas J. Jennings to Mrs. Maria Dufoe, February 25, 1863, Thomas J. Jennings Letters, Southern Historical Collection.
[26] Rawick, The American Slave . . . North Carolina Narratives, Part I, 65.
[27] George F. Winston to a friend or neighbor, February 15, 1863, New Bern Occupation Papers; "Corporal," Letters from the Forty-fourth Regiment M.V.M., 48-49.

A number of skilled artisans who had resided in New Bern as free blacks prior to the Civil War joined with the town's contrabands in entering trades and undertaking various jobs during the Federal occupation. Shown above is a blacksmith and wheelwright shop operated by the freedmen of New Bern. Engraving from Colyer, *Report of the Services Rendered by the Freed People*, p. 11.

Among the population of New Bern were a number of free blacks. Some of them had lived there as freemen before the war and had remained when the Federals captured the town in 1862. Skilled free blacks and slaves joined the New Bern contrabands in entering trades and undertaking jobs in and around the city. They became carpenters, caulkers, shipwrights, blacksmiths, masons, shoemakers, coopers, mill-wrights, engineers, carriage makers, painters, barbers, tailors, draymen, grocers, cooks, hucksters, butchers, gardeners, fishermen, oystermen, sailors, boatmen, and preachers. One officer testified that some of these people "were becoming rich; all are doing well for themselves, even in these times."[28]

The occupation of the North Carolina coastal region by the Union army led the Lincoln administration in 1862 to initiate the political reconstruction of the area. This work was launched simultaneously with reconstruction efforts in other Confederate areas occupied by Federal troops—western Tennessee, northwestern Arkansas, and the New Orleans district of Louisiana. Lincoln, who had consistently denied the legality of secession, hoped that once the citizens of states occupied by Federal forces had organized "loyal" governments, those states or portions thereof could be restored to the Union. To achieve this end in North Carolina, the president in May, 1862, appointed Edward Stanly as pro-

---

[28] Horace James, *Annual Report of the Superintendent of Negro Affairs in North Carolina, 1864. With an Appendix, Containing the History and Management of the Freedmen in this Department up to June 1st, 1865* (Boston: W. P. Brown, Printers, n.d.), 10-12, hereinafter cited as James, *Annual Report of the Superintendent of Negro Affairs in North Carolina, 1864.*

visional governor of that portion of the state, including New Bern and its vicinity, under Federal control.[29]

Stanly had been born in New Bern in 1810 and had practiced law in the state. He was a member of the United States Congress from 1837 to 1843 and during the 1840s had served in the North Carolina legislature, was speaker of the state House of Commons, and also served as state attorney general. In 1849 he returned to Congress for two terms and in 1853 moved to San Francisco, where he practiced law and was the Republican candidate for governor of California in 1857.[30]

President Lincoln hoped that as provisional governor, Stanly could create a loyal civil government that would provide security and leadership for Union sympathizers throughout the state. From Lincoln's point of view, Stanly was a good choice to stimulate Union sentiment in North Carolina. He had strong Union sympathies and was well known by the people and leaders of the state.[31]

Stanly was not, however, sympathetic to the plight of the freed slaves within his jurisdiction. After assuming office in May, 1862, he took measures that brought him in conflict with Vincent Colyer and others who were laboring to improve the condition of blacks in New Bern. Although the provisional governor approved of Colyer's efforts to feed and clothe contrabands as well as white refugees, he adamantly opposed educating the blacks and instead ordered the superintendent to close the evening schools. Stanly's explanation for this action was that he had "been sent to restore the old order of things," which meant that he was obliged to enforce the antebellum state laws concerning blacks. In opposing black education, he cited a prewar North Carolina law that prohibited the teaching of reading or writing to slaves.[32]

Stanly also became involved in the return of a fugitive slave girl to her owner, Nicholas Bray, who lived two miles from New Bern. The incident caused panic among the fugitive slaves in New Bern, and many of them hid in nearby swamps and other places to avoid being returned to their masters. A correspondent for the *New York Times* reported: "One old man of sixty told me to-day that he would rather be placed before a cannon and blown to pieces than go back. Multitudes say they would rather die."

Stanly's actions in closing the schools and in the "Bray affair" outraged antislavery advocates both in the northern states and among the

---

[29] Brown, *Edward Stanly*, 202-203.
[30] *Biographical Directory of the American Congress, 1774-1971 . . .* (Washington: Government Printing Office, 1971), 1743.
[31] Brown, *Edward Stanly*, 2-3.
[32] Barrett, *Civil War in North Carolina*, 127-128.

14

New England troops stationed in New Bern. To protest Stanly's actions, Colyer went to Washington, D.C., where he received support from Radical Republicans and abolitionists such as Senator Charles Sumner of Massachusetts. He also had an interview with President Lincoln, who, according to Colyer's account, assured him that he had given no instructions to Stanly to enforce the prewar laws of North Carolina and declared that no fugitive slaves would be returned to their masters. On June 24 Colyer returned to New Bern and reopened his schools. When he adopted a conciliatory policy toward Stanly, the governor promised not to interfere with the schools.[33]

Many of the New England troops felt that Colyer had made a good start in his efforts to help the freedmen, but they eventually came to believe that he was neglecting his responsibilities to blacks, especially in light of his attempts to placate Stanly. Colyer confessed that he was directing more of his efforts toward aiding destitute whites, who might have been counted as possible Union supporters, than toward his black charges. Such action found favor with Stanly, who held that reconstruction to the Union should be achieved only with support for and by white loyalists.

Partly as a result of the army's disillusionment with him, Colyer left New Bern with General Burnside when the latter was transferred to the Army of the Potomac in the fall of 1862. When Colyer departed, Major General John G. Foster, Burnside's successor, appointed army chaplain James Means to the position of superintendent of the poor.[34] Stanly remained as provisional governor until 1863, when he resigned in protest at the issuance of the Emancipation Proclamation.[35]

The slaves of North Carolina generally understood the meaning of the proclamation and were prepared to avail themselves of the new life it offered. George F. Winston witnessed this attitude among the blacks who came within the Federal lines. "We visited one family in particular," he wrote back to Massachusetts,

where several times we enjoyed breakfasts of which the principal portion was corn cake. They were very intelligent and although they could neither read nor

---

[33] Brown, *Edward Stanly*, 208-213.

[34] Bell I. Wiley, *Southern Negroes, 1861-1865* (New York: Holt, Rinehart and Winston, second edition, 1953), 205, hereinafter cited as Wiley, *Southern Negroes*; *Freedmen's Advocate* (New York), March, 1864, hereinafter cited as *Freedmen's Advocate*; R. N. Scott and others (eds.), *The War of the Rebellion: A Compilation of the Official Records of the Union and Confederate Armies* (Washington: Government Printing Office, 70 volumes, 1880-1901), Series I, IX, 411, hereinafter cited as *Official Records (Army)*; Benjamin Quarles, *The Negro in the Civil War* (Boston: Little, Brown and Company, 1953), 164-165, hereinafter cited as Quarles, *The Negro in the Civil War*.

[35] Barrett, *Civil War in North Carolina*, 173-174.

write, yet had ideas upon matters pertaining to themselves, & very correct ones too. They are quite well informed upon the President's proclamation at least the portion relating to their immediate change of condition, viz. freedom. There is no use in repeating that they are not capable of taking care of themselves, and that they do not desire their freedom, for it is wholly false. Necessity alone would soon teach them the former invention. The fact that all of them who can run away from their masters is a sufficient answer to the latter assertion.[36]

Not only did the Emancipation Proclamation offer the slaves of the Confederacy a promise of freedom but it also gave them the opportunity to fight for that freedom. Soon after the issuance of the proclamation, the recruitment of black soldiers into the Union army began in New Bern. For some time the use of black soldiers to aid the Union war effort had been on the minds of many Federal officers and government officials, including President Lincoln. A number of Union officers were opposed to allowing blacks to serve as soldiers, but many others felt that such a measure was a means by which the Confederacy could be significantly hurt economically and militarily. In the fall of 1862 some officers, such as General Benjamin F. Butler, then stationed in Louisiana, began to make limited use of blacks as soldiers. At the same time, black troops were also used experimentally in Kansas, Missouri, and at some points along the Atlantic coast.[37]

In New Bern the former bondsmen were no longer content to be restricted to serving as laborers or servants for the fighting men. Instead, they desired to don the blue uniforms with the brass buttons they admired so much and bear arms in the defense of their liberty.

In April, 1863, Secretary of War Edwin M. Stanton authorized Colonel Edward A. Wild of Boston to organize a brigade of black troops in the Department of North Carolina. This unit, which came to be known as the "African Brigade," was composed of three regiments of blacks from North Carolina and one regiment (the Fifty-fifth Massachusetts) of northern blacks. Wild was given the rank of brigadier general and stationed in New Bern, where he undertook to enlist black recruits from among former slaves. Blacks responded immediately to his appeals.[38] "Recruiting for the African Brigade is progressing lively," wrote Corporal Z. T. Haines. "Quite a recruiting fever has seized the freedmen of New Bern." An officer noted that "the able-bodied men mostly enlist."

---

[36] George F. Winston to a friend or neighbor, February 15, 1863, New Bern Occupation Papers.

[37] Dudley Taylor Cornish, *The Sable Arm: Negro Troops in the Union Army, 1861-1865* (New York: Longmans, Green and Company, 1956), x-xii, 56-57, hereinafter cited as Cornish, *The Sable Arm.*

[38] Cornish, *The Sable Arm,* 129-130.

In April, 1863, Colonel Edward A. Wild of Boston was authorized to organize a brigade of black troops in the Department of North Carolina. New Bern blacks responded willingly to Wild's recruitment efforts. Shown above are a number of black volunteers passing New Bern's Broad Street Episcopal Church. Engraving from *Frank Leslie's Illustrated Newspaper*, XVII (February 27, 1864).

The training performance of the new men-at-arms was, on the whole, impressive, and they responded well to discipline, accepted responsibility, and acquired the other virtues of good soldiers. "Our black recruits," reported Haines, "are industriously drilling in marching and the manual. [They] are already winning golden opinions for their soldierly qualities. Our most bitter negropholists [sic] admit that they will fight. ..."[39] Although the Lincoln government originally intended to utilize "colored soldiers" only for garrison duty, the necessities of war soon required that they be used in combat.

It took special courage for many of the former slaves to enlist, for upon hearing of the Federal policy to recruit Negroes, Confederates vowed to treat captured black troops as insurrectionists, not prisoners of war. Subsequently in some battles, such as that at Fort Pillow, Tennessee, in 1864, Confederate soldiers summarily executed and massacred black soldiers who surrendered or were captured. In addition the Confederate secretary of war ordered that Union officers who

---

[39] "Corporal," *Letters from the Forty-fourth Regiment M.V.M.*, 95; James, *Annual Report of the Superintendent of Negro Affairs in North Carolina, 1864*, 6.

17

To most freedmen, service in the United States Army was a "bold renunciation of the stigma of slavery" and a source of considerable pride. Engraving from *Pictorial War Record*, III (September 29, 1883), p. 37.

trained and led black soldiers were to be executed when taken prisoners.[40]

Many freedmen viewed service in the army as a bold renunciation of the stigma of slavery and an initial step toward an assertion of manhood and a better place in society. They were as proud of their new status as fighting men as they were of their uniforms. When General Wild's brigade departed New Bern for duty in South Carolina on July 30, 1863, it proudly bore a beautiful banner that it had received from the Colored Ladies Union Relief Association, which had collected funds for the banner "from their own people" in New Bern.[41]

In South Carolina the soldiers of the brigade participated in General Quincy Adams Gillmore's unsuccessful attempt to take Fort Wagner, the key defense point for Charleston. Although they left New Bern for South Carolina in such haste that they were forced to leave behind most of their camp equipment, they spent most of the campaign on Folly Island, where they saw little action.[42]

After the brigade left Folly Island in October, 1863, two regiments traveled to Norfolk, Virginia, where General Benjamin F. Butler, who had replaced General Foster in command of the Department of Virginia and North Carolina, ordered them into the northeastern counties of North Carolina. The purposes of the expedition were to reopen navigation on the Dismal Swamp Canal, to protect Union inhabitants plundered by Confederate guerrillas, and to entice as many slaves as possible away from their owners and procure recruits from among the escapees.

The black troops acquitted themselves well during this raid. General Wild reported that they freed about 2,500 slaves, burned four guerrilla

[40] *Official Records (Army)*, Series I, XXVIII, Part II, 73; Cornish, *The Sable Arm*, 95-96.
[41] Quarles, *The Negro in the Civil War*, 247.
[42] *Official Records (Army)*, Series I, XXVIII, Part II, 73.

During a December, 1863, raid into northeastern North Carolina, two regiments of General Wild's African Brigade "acquitted themselves well." Shown in this engraving are Wild (on horseback at center), his black troops, and a number of slaves liberated during the raid. Many of the soldiers in the brigade resided at the Trent River settlement. Engraving from the files of the Division of Archives and History.

camps, captured over fifty guns along with much ammunition and equipment, took a number of prisoners, hanged one guerrilla, captured four large boats engaged in the transportation of war contraband, and took many horses. The raid was important because it was the first "of any magnitude undertaken [solely] by negro troops since their enlistment was authorized by Congress." A northern reporter who accompanied the expedition was impressed with the soldiers' performance and concluded that "by it the question of their efficiency in any branch of the service has been practically set at rest." The Negro troops, he reported, were "thoroughly obedient to their officers [and] performed in the enemy's country all the duties of white soldiers—scouting, skirmishing, picket duty, guard duty, every service incident to the occupation of hostile towns, and best of all, fighting." Black soldiers of North Carolina were to demonstrate further their courage and fighting ability at New Bern during two attempts by the Confederates to retake the town in March, 1863, and February, 1864.[43]

Perhaps the North Carolina soldier best remembered for his service in the African Brigade was First Sergeant Furney Bryant. Bryant had

---

[43] Barrett, *Civil War in North Carolina*, 177-179; Frank Moore (ed.), *The Rebellion Record: A Diary of American Events, with Documents, Narratives, Illustrative Incidents, Poetry, Etc.* (New York: D. Von Nostrand, 11 volumes, 1869), VIII, 304, quoted in Barrett, *Civil War in North Carolina*, 180.

Furney Bryant, a former slave who came to New Bern as a refugee "in rags" (left), attended Vincent Colyer's schools, learned to read and write, and later enlisted in the black First North Carolina Regiment. As a soldier (right) Bryant won promotion to the rank of first sergeant for his intelligence and leadership. Engravings from Colyer, *Report of the Services Rendered by the Freed People*, pp. 13 and 14 respectively.

been a slave who fled "in rags" to New Bern. Although destitute and illiterate, he attended Superintendent Vincent Colyer's schools, learned to read and write, and served as a spy for the army. He enlisted in the black First North Carolina Regiment and accompanied his unit during the Charleston expedition. There he was promoted to first sergeant for his display of intelligence and leadership. On a furlough in 1864 he visited in New York former superintendent Colyer, who had come to that city to aid those blacks who had felt the wrath of northerners during the New York Draft Riots. "The contrast in his personal appearance, in his new suit of army blue," wrote Colyer, upon seeing Bryant, "was not more remarkable than the ... letter received from him ... proves his growth in the knowledge of letters to be. Let no one say that freedom is not better than slavery, with such examples before them." Along with other black soldiers, Bryant distinguished himself in February, 1864, when the Confederates launched an all-out attack to recapture New Bern.[44]

Yet, as has been seen, freedom was only the first step for thousands of slaves seeking new lives in a world turned upside down by the holocaust of war. Having escaped their old way of life, often with little more than

---

[44] Colyer, *Report of the Services Rendered by the Freed People*, 13-14, 18.

the clothes on their backs, these former bondsmen faced an uncertain and possibly bleak future as illiterate, unskilled, and penniless freedmen. As the war progressed and the likelihood of Confederate victory waned, North Carolina slaves became aware of the improbability that their owners might recapture and punish them. Consequently, in ever increasing numbers they left their masters and sought freedom and Federal protection in New Bern.

By early 1863 the number of blacks coming to the city had reached an alarming level and continued to grow daily. Colyer had left the state, and his successor, the Reverend James Means, an army chaplain, soon died of yellow fever. General Foster searched among his officers for the man most qualified to assume responsibility for the thousands of fugitive slaves whose numbers had been growing in the past few months. The officer he selected in January was the Reverend Horace James, a chaplain from Massachusetts. James had greater responsibility for and consequently a more lasting impact on the freedmen of New Bern, both during and immediately following the Civil War, than either of his predecessors. Colyer had made a significant beginning in providing aid for displaced slaves, but his tenure as superintendent was short—about four months. Also, as Colyer himself admitted, the duties of his office forced him to spend most of his time caring for the needs of white soldiers and destitute civilians. James was the first officer specifically appointed superintendent of Negro affairs (and after March, 1865, the assistant commissioner of the Freedmen's Bureau) in North Carolina.[45]

Before the war James had served as pastor of Old South Congregational Church in Worcester. He joined the Twenty-fifth Infantry Regiment of Massachusetts as a chaplain on October 28, 1861, and accompanied the unit to Virginia, where he served under General Benjamin Butler at Fortress Monroe. There he gained his first experience working in behalf of escaped slaves. In 1862 his regiment was part of the Burnside expedition, which captured Roanoke Island, and he was placed in charge of the numerous contrabands who sought refuge within the Union lines. In March, 1862, the Twenty-fifth Regiment participated in the capture of New Bern, and James, while serving as chaplain, soon established evening schools for blacks. He also gave religious instruction

[45] George R. Bentley, *A History of the Freedmen's Bureau* (Philadelphia: University of Pennsylvania, 1955; reprinted New York: Octagon Books, 1970), 25, hereinafter cited as Bentley, *History of the Freedmen's Bureau*; Wiley, *Southern Negroes*, 205; *Official Records (Army)*, Series, I, IX, 411.

and solicited food and clothing from northern philanthropic organizations, largely on his own initiative.[46]

It was because of James's past experience with contrabands that General Foster appointed him to the new post of superintendent of Negro affairs in Federally occupied North Carolina. At that time the United States government was beginning to direct more effort toward the relief of blacks and destitute whites in the South; this led eventually to the creation of the Bureau of Refugees, Freedmen, and Abandoned Lands (the Freedmen's Bureau) in March, 1865.

Like his predecessors, James was responsible for taking censuses of black refugees in eastern North Carolina and for finding them employment. He was further encumbered with the responsibility of issuing rations, medicine, and clothing to destitute freedmen. Moreover, he was obliged to supervise the making of contracts between former slaves and whites and to ensure that those agreements were faithfully executed by both parties. Working with the assistance of New England philanthropic organizations, he made tremendous strides in providing educational opportunities for blacks.[47]

In order to provide the many destitute freedmen in eastern North Carolina with places to live as well as to establish secure locations in which to implement his programs, James decided to create a number of refugee camps on land that had been abandoned or was in the possession of the United States government. At these camps James hoped to provide temporary aid in the form of food and shelter for black families until they could become self-sufficient through the programs he planned to establish. These programs included basic education, vocational training, and the creation of small industries to utilize black labor. Camps were necessary, James thought, because the Union army controlled so little land in North Carolina on which to place the blacks. "We control indeed a broad area of navigable waters, and command the approaches from the sea," he remarked, "but have scarcely room enough on land to spread

---

[46] Samuel H. Putnam, *The Story of Company A, Twenty-fifth Regiment, Mass. Vols. in the War of the Rebellion* (Worcester, Mass.: Putnam, Davis and Company, 1886), 117, hereinafter cited as Putnam, *The Story of Company A*; *Massachusetts Soldiers, Sailors, and Marines in the Civil War* (Norwood, Mass.: Norwood Press, 8 volumes plus index, 1931-1935), III, 3, hereinafter cited as *Massachusetts Soldiers, Sailors, and Marines*; Charles Emery Stevens, *Worcester Churches, 1719-1889* (Worcester, Mass.: Lucius Paulinus Goddard, 1890), 22.

[47] *Freedmen's Advocate*, March, 1864; Wiley, *Southern Negroes*, 204; Nancy Smith Linthicum, "The American Missionary Association and North Carolina Freedmen, 1863-1868" (unpublished master's thesis, North Carolina State University, Raleigh, 1977), 44, hereinafter cited as Linthicum, "The American Missionary Association and North Carolina Freedmen."

our tents upon. If land had been accessible on which to settle the Negroes, it would have prevented huddling them together in the fortified towns and temporary camps. But there was left to us no alternative." Because so much of the state was still under Confederate control, those escaped slaves who attempted to settle and farm outside of Union-occupied towns and freedmen camps were often recaptured, killed, or driven by Confederate troops back to areas under Federal protection.[48]

James began his work in North Carolina by establishing on Roanoke Island a freedmen's camp that he hoped would serve as a model for future black colonies. He then made a journey to the North, where he raised $9,000 with which to buy supplies and equipment and to hire several teachers for the black refugees. He cleared land on the island and assigned plots to the former slaves. With the aid of a sawmill that James had purchased, blacks on Roanoke Island built their own homes and several schools. Some of them learned trades such as spinning, weaving, barrel making, shoemaking, shingle splitting, and fishing. Others worked for the army. By the end of the war the black population on the island totaled about 3,000. James also established smaller camps in other areas on the coast, including Beaufort, Carolina City, Washington, and Plymouth.[49]

As mentioned previously, New Bern presented James with his greatest problem because of its large and rapidly growing black population, one fourth of which was dependent upon the United States government for support. New Bern remained the chief center for black refugees inasmuch as the Union headquarters and the greatest number of Federal troops were located there, and in close proximity to the town there was sufficient land on which to settle the freedmen. In the spring of 1863 James established a settlement about one and a half miles south of New Bern at the confluence of the Neuse and Trent rivers. The land he selected had once belonged to Richard Dobbs Spaight, who had served as governor of North Carolina from 1792 to 1795 and had been a member of the federal Constitutional Convention of 1787. In 1802 Spaight was killed in a duel with John Stanly, a former congressman and a native of New Bern (and father of Provisional Governor Edward Stanly).[50] The

[48] James, *Annual Report of the Superintendent of Negro Affairs in North Carolina, 1864*, 3-4; Wiley, *Southern Negroes*, 207.

[49] Wiley, *Southern Negroes*, 206.

[50] Bentley, *History of the Freedmen's Bureau*, 63; *News and Observer* (Raleigh), April 26, 1893, hereinafter cited as *News and Observer*; Beth G. Crabtree, *North Carolina Governors, 1585-1975* (Raleigh: Division of Archives and History, Department of Cultural Resources, third printing, revised, 1974), 52-53.

Spaight lands had descended through the governor's heirs to Confederate Colonel Peter G. Evans of New Bern, who commanded the Sixty-third Regiment, North Carolina Troops. The Confederate army had used the tract early in the war as a camp for soldiers, and the Union army acquired the property "by military orders and occupancy" after capturing New Bern in 1862. Once the freedmen were settled on the site, Federal authorities called it the Trent River settlement or the Trent River camp.[51]

The camp was one of three established in the New Bern area. But when Confederate forces under General George E. Pickett attacked New Bern in late January, 1864, the other two camps, which were located outside of the Union fortifications, had to be abandoned. According to James, "this made it manifest that the colored people were not safe in their camps. A number of them were captured within two miles of the city, some were killed, and all were driven from their homes."

As a result of the Confederate invasion, General John J. Peck, then commanding the Union forces in North Carolina, ordered James to consolidate all three camps at the Trent River settlement, which being within the Federal perimeter was reasonably secure from Confederate attack. "It was immediately done," James recalled. "Streets were run out, and lots assigned, fifty feet by sixty, allowing a little garden spot to each house." The settlement originally encompassed about 30 acres and included 800 houses, most of which were cabins constructed of "shakes," short boards from 4 to 5 feet long and split by hand. The camp was first put under the charge of one L. J. Howell, a northern white man, "whose ability and tact make him a valuable helper in Negro affairs." In 1864 2,798 freedmen lived in the camp, 1,226 of whom received "help from the government as dependents." A number of the freedmen who had families in the camp were members of the African Brigade. Others found work with the army or held odd jobs.[52]

A census taken by James in January of that year revealed that a total

---

[51] Brevet Lieutenant Colonel Jacob F. Chur to Major General Oliver Otis Howard, December 4, 1866, Endorsements Sent, Records of Bureau of Refugees, Freedmen, and Abandoned Lands for North Carolina, Record Group 105, National Archives, Washington, D.C., hereinafter cited as Freedmen's Bureau Records, RG 105; Louis H. Manarin and Weymouth T. Jordan, Jr. (eds.), *North Carolina Troops, 1861-1865: A Roster* (Raleigh: Division of Archives and History [projected multivolume series, 1966—]), II, 372; Report of Captain Horace James for the Eastern District [of North Carolina] for the Quarter ending September 30, 1865, Records Relating to Lands and Property, Statistical Land Reports, July, 1865-December, 1868, Freedmen's Bureau Records, RG 105.

[52] James, *Annual Report of the Superintendent of Negro Affairs in North Carolina, 1864*, 7-8; Bentley, *History of the Freedmen's Bureau*, 63; Report of Captain Horace James for the Eastern District for the Quarter ending September 30, 1865, Freedmen's Bureau Records, RG 105.

of 17,419 blacks were under the protection of the Union forces in eastern. North Carolina. Of these, 8,591 were located in New Bern and its vicinity. In January, 1865, there were 10,782 former slaves in the New Bern area, about 6,000 of whom resided in the town. James estimated that only one sixth of the black population had been residents before the war. Those freedmen at New Bern who were not employed by the government but were instead engaged in their own occupations earned a combined yearly income of $151,562. The number who reported an income of $500 to $1,000 was 110. Eighteen freedmen made over $1,000, four over $2,000, and two over $3,000 per year.[53] (See Appendix, Tables 1, 2, and 3.)

When General William T. Sherman and his troops marched through North Carolina during the last weeks of the Civil War, additional thousands of slaves followed him into the state from the south. Five thousand came to the New Bern area, and many of them died as a result of hardship and disease. In the wake of this late influx the size of the Trent River camp swelled to about 3,000 blacks.[54]

Conditions had been primitive in the Trent River settlement when it was first established in 1863. By the end of the war, however, James pointed with pride at the improvement in the camp. In January, 1865, he noted that in addition to the shacks of the freedmen, the settlement consisted of a number of other buildings, including the bureau headquarters, a school, a blacksmith shop, a hospital, and several churches. He also reported that the individual gardens were productive and that the camp residents sometimes sold vegetables to white refugees who lived in "a neighboring camp, composed of better houses and standing on better soil," but "neglected to raise anything themselves." The corn was at times 15 feet high and overtopped the cabins. James boasted that "if we must have camps, or African villages, in which temporarily to shelter and feed refugees from bondage, this settlement, located healthfully on the banks of the Trent, is a model for imitation."[55]

As the war drew to a close the camp was renamed James City to honor the man who had established it. For the next few years the settlement would be called by all three names: Trent River settlement, Trent River camp, or James City. The last name, however, would be the one ultimately to survive.

---

[53] James, *Annual Report of the Superintendent of Negro Affairs in North Carolina, 1864,* 3-4, 11-12.

[54] Wiley, *Southern Negroes,* 207; Captain Horace James to Lieutenant Fred H. Beecher, September 20, 1865, Letters Received, Freedmen's Bureau Records, RG 105.

[55] James, *Annual Report of the Superintendent of Negro Affairs in North Carolina, 1864,* 8.

II. HORACE JAMES

For a long time prior to coming to North Carolina the Reverend Horace James had cherished the idealistic hope of improving the condition of blacks in the South. Like many antebellum New Englanders and other northerners, he was opposed to the institution of slavery and felt strongly that it should be abolished. He was not, however, an abolitionist, which has been defined by historian James M. McPherson as one of "those Americans who before the Civil War had agitated for immediate, unconditional, and universal abolition of slavery in the United States."[1] Although James had attacked the system from a pulpit in Massachusetts before the Civil War, he had hoped that "all at the South and at the North would examine Negro slavery, not with fanatical zeal, but with calm, considerate attention, and agree together to put an end to it by gradual and compensated emancipation, as a harbinger and hostage of our peace, and a blessed deliverance both to the master and the slave."[2]

Despite his hope for a calm, gradual emancipation, James was adamant that slavery should not be allowed to expand into the territories that had been acquired by the United States during the Mexican War; and he had spoken vehemently against the passage of the Kansas-Nebraska Act in 1854. Two years later he made a speech in Massachusetts that deplored the beating received by abolitionist Senator Charles Sumner of Massachusetts at the hands of South Carolina Representative Preston S. Brooks. (Sumner's heated attack on slavery in the territories and his insulting remarks hurled at Brooks's slaveholding uncle, Senator Andrew P. Butler of South Carolina, led to the assault.) Like Sumner and many members of the new Republican party, James wanted slavery abolished in the District of Columbia, a revision of the fugitive slave law to allow trial by jury, and the abolition of the domestic slave trade. When the war came, James, like Abraham Lincoln, considered the goal of the Federal effort to be the restoration of the

---

[1] James M. McPherson, *The Struggle for Equality: Abolitionists and the Negro in the Civil War and Reconstruction* (Princeton, N.J.: Princeton University Press, 1964), 3.

[2] Horace James, *Our Duties to the Slave: A Sermon Preached before the Original Congregational Church and Society in Wrentham, Mass., on Thanksgiving Day, November 28, 1846* (Boston: Richardson and Filmer, 1847), passim, hereinafter cited as James, *Our Duties to the Slave*; Horace James, *An Oration Delivered in Newbern, North Carolina, before the Twenty-fifth Regiment, Massachusetts Volunteers, July 4, 1862* (Boston: W. F. Brown and Company, 1862), 27, hereinafter cited as James, *An Oration Delivered in Newbern*.

Horace James (1818-1875) was appointed superintendent of Negro affairs in Federally occupied North Carolina in January, 1863. He served in this capacity, and later as an official of the Freedmen's Bureau, until December, 1865. Near the close of the Civil War the Trent River settlement came to be known as James City, an honor bestowed upon James for his many contributions to the welfare of the freedmen who resided there. Photograph from a copy in the North Carolina Collection, University of North Carolina library, Chapel Hill.

Union and not necessarily the immediate abolition of slavery in the South.[3]

But as the war progressed, James changed his opinion about the North's purpose in the conflict. He expressed this change of sentiment in 1862 while delivering a Fourth of July speech to his regiment in New Bern. In an effort to explain to the troops the reason for the conflict, he announced that the Union army was fighting for a noble cause; and although the war had commenced as an effort to preserve the federal Union, it had soon taken on a greater connotation—the defense of human liberty. James asserted that the elimination of slavery, not merely the restoration of the Union, must thereafter be a major goal of the northern war effort. "We have not," he declared, "introduced the negro into this war. But he is in it, and in every part of it, and can no more be expelled from it than leaven can be removed from the loaf that has begun to ferment." James insisted that in order to vindicate the United States in the eyes of God and the rest of the world, the war must thereafter become a righteous crusade to end black servitude: "Aye, we aim at a union purified. It does not wholly satisfy us that its integrity is to be maintained, we long to see it improved and strengthened in every

[3] Franklin P. Rice, *The Worcester Book: A Diary of Noteworthy Events in Worcester, Massachusetts, From 1657 to 1883* (Worcester: Putnam, Davis and Company, 1884), 30, 60; Eric Foner, *Free Soil, Free Labor, Free Men: The Ideology of the Republican Party before the Civil War* (New York: Oxford University Press, 1970), 211-225; James, *Our Duties to the Slave*, 15-20.

element that enters into material greatness. Why stint and limit an organization so superior, so freighted with sublime possibilities, so well fitted, as experience shows, to shed a blessed light upon the nations that sit in darkness, and be an element of hope to the world?"[4] Through his direct exposure to the institution of slavery and the human beings who fled from it and as a result of his experience in aiding slaves at Fortress Monroe and coastal North Carolina, James had abandoned his former theories on gradual emancipation.

James's experience in caring for black refugees at the Trent River settlement and elsewhere during the Civil War also convinced him that, contrary to the opinions of many whites, North and South, former slaves were capable of a transition from the dependency of slavery to a state of self-sufficiency and responsibility. His exposure, then, to the realities of war and the complex problem of aiding fugitive slaves did not lessen James's commitment to the antislavery cause. Rather, the reality of the situation impelled him to view slavery as a sin and to advocate abolition on grounds of morality.

While working as superintendent of Negro affairs and later as assistant commissioner of the Freedmen's Bureau in North Carolina, James developed definite ideas about the capacity and ability of blacks. In 1865 he summarized his views and admitted that "the experience of the last year has confirmed me in some opinions which a previous sojourn of two years in North Carolina had suggested." He wrote that Negroes were not as helpless or dependent as the poor whites who came under his care. The black refugees, he felt, were more physically active, industrious, and religious than their white counterparts. But as did most white men of his time, James apparently accepted the premise that whites were biologically and intellectually superior to blacks. He also viewed miscegenation as a detriment to blacks as well as whites and declared that it weakened both races.[5]

According to James, the former slaves were well aware of the advantages that freedom offered over bondage. "The negroes are grateful for liberty," he announced, "and but little inclined to abuse it. They know as we do not what slavery means and are truly grateful that they have escaped it." Yet they were not inclined toward vengeance on whites for their former condition. "Devout thankfulness to God is their prevailing sentiment."

---

[4] James, *An Oration Delivered in Newbern*, 24-25.
[5] James, *Annual Report of the Superintendent of Negro Affairs in North Carolina, 1864*, 44.

28

Religious activity played such a large part in their lives, James observed, "that almost the only comfort they enjoyed under slavery was derived from this source. It may be that their changed condition will train them into the vices of a higher state of Christian society and make profanity, drunkenness and crime among them as it is, alas, among the dominant race. But we hope not." James was opposed to exposing the freedmen to the evils of alcohol and had been a strong antiliquor advocate in Massachusetts; at one time he was treasurer of the Worcester Temperance League. He strictly forbade the use of alcoholic spirits in James City.

The superintendent commented on the degree of respect and devotion that the freedmen continued to show the Union soldiers "who have brought them deliverance." "Abraham Lincoln," James wrote, "is to them the chiefest among ten thousand, and altogether lovely. They mingle his name with their prayers and their praises evermore." James also noted that the former slaves were anticipating their new status as citizens and the full political, educational, and legal rights that citizenship entailed.[6]

Beginning during the war, James gave education the highest priority among his programs to help former slaves survive as free people in a society controlled by whites. He worked hard to ensure that all the freedmen under his supervision had the opportunity for secular and religious instruction. He felt that it was important that the Freedmen's Bureau do as much work as possible to establish education for blacks before the military forces were withdrawn from the state and the freedmen were left alone to deal with their former masters.[7]

Under James's supervision, by May, 1863, thirty-two soldiers were serving as teachers for 485 "scholars" in Sunday schools and 328 students at a day school in New Bern. Shortly afterward, James opened two new schools for blacks, which were taught by female teachers from two benevolent societies—the American Missionary Association and the New England Freedmen's Aid Society. These were the first regular schools for blacks in North Carolina, which opened their doors on July 23, 1863, in two black churches in New Bern. Soon thereafter, the National Freedmen's Relief Association likewise established a school for

---

[6] James, *Annual Report of the Superintendent of Negro Affairs in North Carolina, 1864*, 44-47; *Evening Gazette* (Worcester, Massachusetts), June 10, 1875, hereinafter cited as *Evening Gazette*.

[7] Linthicum, "The American Missionary Association and North Carolina Freedmen," 95; James, *Annual Report of the Superintendent of Negro Affairs in North Carolina, 1864*, 44.

Shown in this engraving is the interior of a typical school established by the Freedmen's Bureau during the Civil War. Note the presence of adult blacks in the classroom. From J. T. Trowbridge, *The South: A Tour of Its Battle-Fields and Ruined Cities, A Journey through the Desolated States, and Talks with the People* (Hartford, Conn.: L. Stebbins, 1866), facing p. 338.

blacks in the town, and all three schools held both day and evening classes under James's watchful eye.[8]

By early 1864 James was supervising 46 northern schoolteachers in North Carolina. Largely through his efforts 26 schools had been opened, 11 of them in New Bern and 5 in the Trent River camp. By the end of the war there were 68 teachers in North Carolina—56 females and 12 males. With the exception of two who were self-supporting, these teachers were salaried members of the benevolent societies. Among the teachers were four blacks, including one woman.[9] (See Appendix, Table 4.)

James thought highly of these teachers and their diligence in the task of educating the former slaves. "No arithmetic can compute the amount of blessing conferred by these sixty-eight teachers, even in this brief period [1864-1865]," he boasted. The teachers endured considerable hardship, particularly in the form of low and often overdue pay, white hostility, and disease. One black teacher, Robert Morrow, who had fled to New Bern early in the war and later fell victim to yellow fever on

[8] James, *Annual Report of the Superintendent of Negro Affairs in North Carolina, 1864*, 39, 41; Linthicum, "The American Missionary Association and North Carolina Freedmen," 94-96; Samuel A. Walker Diary, Archives, Division of Archives and History, Raleigh.

[9] James, *Annual Report of the Superintendent of Negro Affairs in North Carolina, 1864*, 41-42.

Roanoke Island, especially impressed James. The superintendent wrote of him:

Robert Morrow at the time of his decease was a sergeant in the 1st North Carolina Heavy Artillery (Colored troops). He came into our lines at the time of an attack upon New Berne, and had been for many years a body servant of the rebel General [James J.] Pettigrew, whom he deserted for liberty and Union. He had a decent education, having been with Pettigrew at West Point, and Chapel Hill, North Carolina, and was an enthusiastic and excellent teacher. He was of pure African blood, had an intellectual cerebral development, and a patriotic heart. He died suddenly, and in his bed, having retired at night as well as usual. He was then engaged in recruiting colored troops at Roanoke Island. It matters little to him that he left the world without warning, for he daily walked with God. He still belongs to the great army which marches under the banner of truth, but he wears a conqueror's wreath and sings the song of victory.[10]

James considered the ownership of land to be just as essential as education to the economic stability of former slaves. After the war he tried unsuccessfully to encourage the federal government to purchase the James City land for the freedmen. At no time, however, did he tell the black residents that the land, which legally remained in the possession of white owners, was theirs to keep, although some freedmen would later claim that he had done so. Like most men of his day, James was committed to laissez faire economics and believed strongly in capitalism and private ownership of property. The idea of the government's giving to one man the property of another, even if the latter was a "rebel" and a slave owner, was more than he could countenance. Such views were reinforced in him by the tenets of New England Calvinism, which held that wealth and property were the natural rewards of good men.[11]

James also had a strong aversion to government aid for those former slaves who were able to support themselves, and he scrupulously supervised the dispensation of government rations to ensure that only the destitute received them. In New Bern and the Trent River settlement he maintained stores for the sale of clothing and other materials donated by benevolent associations. He insisted that those blacks who could afford to pay small sums for clothing should do so, particularly able-bodied men who were employed. The money collected went for services for destitute freedmen. Those without the means to pay, particularly

---

[10] James, *Annual Report of the Superintendent of Negro Affairs in North Carolina, 1864*, 43-44.

[11] James, *Annual Report of the Superintendent of Negro Affairs in North Carolina, 1864*, 45; Captain Horace James to Lieutenant Fred H. Beecher, September 20, 1865, Letters Received, Freedmen's Bureau Records, RG 105; Carl N. Degler, *Out of Our Past: The Forces that Shaped Modern America* (New York: Harper and Row, 1970), 6, 8.

women and children with no income, were given essential clothing from quartermaster stores. James confessed that he often gave away articles slated for sale by the benevolent societies and sold some that were intended to be given away. "We have been guided," he insisted, "by this one rule: 'What will promote the highest welfare of these people?' and in its application have used the best judgment we could summon on the spot." The philanthropic organizations that furnished the clothing approved of his store operations.[12] The *Freedmen's Advocate* of New York applauded his efforts and claimed that the stores saved self-supporting freedmen from the "exorbitant prices of interested traders & sellers— unfeeling tradesmen."[13]

James never wavered in his belief in the ability of slaves to succeed as free people, but he frequently expressed exasperation at the many difficulties and setbacks he and the freedmen encountered in their efforts to make the transition from slavery. Sometimes he lost patience with the slow progress of the former slaves at the Trent River settlement. James did not blame this lack of immediate accomplishment on inherent racial characteristics but instead maintained that slavery had done little to prepare blacks for success as free people. He insisted that the freedmen sometimes appeared lazy only because they associated being free with being rid of manual labor—a concept they had learned as slaves by observing the behavior of their white owners. They "never saw a gentleman work, until the Yankees came here, and before this time their only rule was to do as little as they could" in bondage. James also noted that the freedmen exhibited considerably more motivation when working their own land or at their own trade. Although sometimes discouraged by the slow progress of his efforts to improve the condition of blacks, James kept his commitment to the freedmen. He expressed his ambivalent feelings when he realistically but optimistically wrote of the former slaves: "Their elevation as a race is a work of patience and time. The growth of character is slow, especially if one must unlearn the traditions of a lifetime to prepare him to commence aright."[14]

In 1864 James was discharged as chaplain of the Twenty-fifth Massachusetts Regiment and was immediately commissioned a captain and

---

[12] James, *Annual Report of the Superintendent of Negro Affairs in North Carolina, 1864*, 14; Horace James to George Whipple, September 15, 1863, American Missionary Association Archives, North Carolina Letters, Dillard University, New Orleans, Louisiana (microfilm copies at D. H. Hill Library, North Carolina State University, Raleigh), hereinafter cited as AMA Archives, North Carolina Letters.

[13] *Freedmen's Advocate*, July, 1864.

[14] James, *Annual Report of the Superintendent of Negro Affairs in North Carolina, 1864*, 45, 46.

assistant quartermaster of United States volunteers, while at the same time retaining his position as superintendent of Negro affairs in North Carolina. In March, 1865, Congress established the Bureau of Refugees, Freedmen, and Abandoned Lands to which passed the responsibility for providing aid to destitute former slaves throughout the South. Secretary of War Edwin M. Stanton selected General Oliver Otis Howard as commissioner of this federal agency, which became popularly known as the Freedmen's Bureau. With the creation of the bureau James became the assistant commissioner for North Carolina, an office he held for only a brief time. He soon requested to be relieved of this position because of a concern for his family's health (and possibly his own), a strong desire to return to the pulpit, and an underlying belief that it would not be long before the federal government abolished the Freedmen's Bureau.[15]

To take James's place as the head of the bureau in the Tar Heel State, General Howard appointed Colonel Eliphalet Whittlesey, a member of Howard's staff. Whittlesey arrived from Washington and established a headquarters at Raleigh in July, 1865, and then divided the state into districts to be served by the bureau. Upon Whittlesey's insistent request, James agreed to remain as subassistant commissioner for the bureau's Eastern District (which included the New Bern area) and to lend his experience in dealing with destitute blacks. Whittlesey also appointed James financial agent for the bureau in the state and announced that in compliance with an order of the adjutant general, all military officers in the Department of North Carolina were "to turn over all abandoned lands, tenements, buildings, and other property now in their possession" to James "whenever the said lands, tenements &c. are not needed for military purposes." Despite the additional duties and his already large responsibilities in the Eastern District, the Massachusetts clergyman nevertheless continued his exertions on behalf of the freedmen. His accomplishments at James City were significant enough that it became Whittlesey's "favorite colony."[16]

---

[15] *Massachusetts Soldiers, Sailors, and Marines*, III, 3, VI, 766; Bentley, *History of the Freedmen's Bureau*, 51-52; *Official Records (Army)*, Series I, XLVI, Part III, 1170; Captain Horace James to Colonel Eliphalet Whittlesey, August, 29, 1865, Unregistered Letters Received, and Whittlesey to Major General O. O. Howard, December 3, 1865, Letters Sent, Freedmen's Bureau Records, RG 105.

[16] J. G. de Roulhac Hamilton, *Reconstruction in North Carolina* (New York: Columbia University Press, 1914), 298; Colonel Eliphalet Whittlesey to Major General O. O. Howard, December 3, 1865, and Whittlesey to Brevet Colonel C. A. Cilley, July 28, 1865, Letters Sent, Freedmen's Bureau Records, RG 105; William S. McFeely, *Yankee Stepfather: General O. O. Howard and the Freedmen* (New Haven: Yale University Press, 1968), 82, hereinafter cited as McFeely, *Yankee Stepfather*.

In August, 1865, James once again requested to be relieved of his duties—this time in the Eastern District. Although he had definitely decided that he wanted to sever his connection with the bureau, he was reluctant to abandon his work with the freedmen at James City and other areas in the district. He wrote to Whittlesey that "my private and personal relations to this work cause me much anxiety in spite of myself. Really, never in my life was I so uncertain in what field of endeavor I can accomplish the most good for my country and my God."

He insisted that he wanted to continue to serve his church and fellowman in some capacity and mentioned to Whittlesey several opportunities that might enable him to achieve that end. For example, the American Missionary Association had asked him to be its New England secretary, and some friends wanted him to start a Congregational church in Washington, North Carolina [?]. Furthermore, he told Whittlesey, "my father and aged mother in their infirmity wish me to be near them, and [my father] is anxious that I should take charge of the *Congregationalist*," a church publication.[17]

Not only were James's parents suffering from "infirmity," but apparently his wife also had a health problem. At various intervals Helen James came to New Bern to assist her husband in his work with the freedmen but on several occasions had to return to Massachusetts to rest. In March, 1864, the *Freedmen's Advocate* referred to her as "an efficient aid to him, laboring far beyond her strength." In the following month the same journal noted that she had returned north, "hoping a respite for a few months may be reinvigorating for a new campaign."[18]

During a yellow fever epidemic in New Bern in 1864, James himself fell victim to the disease. William T. Briggs, an official of the American Missionary Association, sat by the clergyman's bed in New Bern one night thinking that the morning would find him dead. "Capt. James," he sadly reported, "has had a relapse & . . . the prospect of his recovery is exceedingly doubtful. I sat with him last night & though not easily discouraged my fears greatly outweigh my hopes. Still I cannot yet believe that such a man will be spared from the field where he is so much needed."[19]

James was a traditional minister of the gospel and, as his speeches and sermons to Union troops indicate, was in his element in the pulpit. He had studied theology at Yale, and after graduating in 1840 took

---

[17] Captain Horace James to Colonel Eliphalet Whittlesey, August 29, 1865, Unregistered Letters Received, Freedmen's Bureau Records, RG 105.

[18] *Freedmen's Advocate*, March, April, 1864.

[19] William T. Briggs to George Whipple, November 25, 1864, AMA Archives, North Carolina Letters.

further theological training at Andover. While serving as a chaplain he preached to Federal soldiers, former slaves, and native whites in both Virginia and coastal North Carolina. In fact, hardly had Federal forces taken New Bern in 1862 than the provost marshal announced that "Rev. Horace James, Chaplain of the 25th Mass. Regt. will conduct Divine Services in the Presbyterian Church in Middle Street, on Sunday, at 11 o'clock." A member of James's regiment recalled that first sermon:

[On] Sunday, March 30th, the whole regiment turned out and marched to church. It was a curious sight—pews filled with Blue Coats and glittering bayonets, six soldiers and six rifles to a pew, darkies peering in at doors and windows, the star spangled banner in one corner, while the Chaplain James in the pulpit completed the picture.[20]

As both a chaplain and an officer of freedmen's affairs during and after the war, James made his Sunday sermons permanent fixtures; and he always harbored a strong desire to return to a traditional role as pastor of a congregation.

' Because James saw himself first and foremost as a minister of the gospel, one of his most pressing ambitions was to establish a Congregational church in North Carolina. He wrote to Whittlesey that if he remained in the state after his resignation from the bureau, he hoped to found such a church in New Bern. He also wanted the church to host lectures given by northern intellectuals. He had already begun efforts to make the New Bern church a reality.[21] "I am not," he wrote to an official of the American Missionary Association on August 10, 1865, "set upon any field of labor in preference to others. If I am not deceived in myself, I want to do just what would build up Zion, bless the world and please God. I want to be in the right place, and the opinion of my brethren on this subject is of great value in making of a decision. Many say I am now in the right place; but the yearnings of my heart and the voice of the spirit . . . within, are toward the ministry. If God would secularize me, whence these aspirations."[22]

Yet James believed that there was still much work to be done for the freedmen at camps like James City and in rural areas of North Carolina. "I feel disposed to stay South a couple of years longer to do this work,"

---

[20] *Evening Gazette*, June 10, 1875; undated newspaper clipping in Henry Toole Clark Scrapbooks, Scrapbook 2, P.C. 235.2, State Archives; Putnam, *The Story of Company A*, 117.
[21] Captain Horace James to Colonel Eliphalet Whittlesey, August 29, 1865, Unregistered Letters Received, Freedmen's Bureau Records, RG 105.
[22] Captain Horace James to Brother Strieby, August 10, 1865, AMA Archives, North Carolina Letters.

he declared in October, 1865, after Whittlesey had convinced him to remain with the bureau a few months more.

Despite these feelings, James interpreted the lack of support for the freedmen's agency by President Andrew Johnson as an indication that the bureau would soon be brought to an end and the former slaves abandoned. Johnson was opposed to the bureau and wanted it dissolved, believing that blacks would fare better with their white employers without the aid of a federal organization and that the support of individual freedmen was outside the function of government.[23] Whittlesey shared his subordinate's opinion and declared in the fall of 1865 that because of the president's position on bureau affairs, "We must contract our operations and be prepared to wind up entirely next spring."[24] Whittlesey had managed to persuade James to remain with the bureau until December, but on the third day of that month he wrote to General Howard that he was sending James's resignation for the commissioner's final approval. "I regret," he wrote,

to lose his service as an officer, but he has remained some months beyond the time when I took his place, and I feel compelled to accede to his wishes. He also promises to remain in the State on other business, & to act as citizen agent of the Bureau without pay. I trust he may be mustered out where he is in accordance with orders which will entitle him to three months entire pay. No officer is more deserving. He has served 4 years doing the hard work of A. Q. M. & Supt. of contrabands nearly all the time, and without promotion of any kind.[25]

With General Howard's acceptance of the resignation, James left the army and his direct association with James City ended, although what subsequently happened to him had an indirect connection with the black settlement.

The "other business" to which Whittlesey referred was James's decision to become associated with a plantation and labor scheme in Pitt County, North Carolina. As part of the plan James became the business

---

[23] Captain Horace James to S. S. Ashley, October 30, 1865, and James to the Secretaries of the American Missionary Association, October 20, 1865, AMA Archives, North Carolina Letters; Bentley, *History of the Freedmen's Bureau*, 103. President Johnson's stubborn refusal to help carry out a Reconstruction policy that included stronger intervention by the United States government in the affairs of the southern states led ultimately to his split with Congress in 1866 and to his subsequent impeachment in 1868. See Eric L. McKitrick, *Andrew Johnson and Reconstruction* (Chicago: University of Chicago Press, 1960), 286-287, hereinafter cited as McKitrick, *Andrew Johnson and Reconstruction*.

[24] Colonel Eliphalet Whittlesey to Captain F. A. Seely, September 25, 1865, Letters Sent, Freedmen's Bureau Records, RG 105.

[25] Colonel Eliphalet Whittlesey to Major General O. O. Howard, December 3, 1865, Letters Sent, Freedmen's Bureau Records, RG 105.

partner of Whittlesey and Winthrop Tappan, a neighbor of Whittlesey in the state of Maine. The plan conceived by Whittlesey and Tappan and presented to James called for the two men from Maine to rent two plantations in Pitt County from the owner, William Grimes. The plantations, named Avon and Yankee Hall, were located about twelve miles from Washington, North Carolina, on opposite sides of the Tar River. James was to receive money for expenses and to have complete charge of the farms, including the hiring and supervision of freedmen as laborers and the purchasing of supplies. The enterprise was to be undertaken for a year, with an option to renew the contract for a second year. While running the plantations, James would also act as a civilian agent for the Freedmen's Bureau in overseeing the laborers employed there. He would receive no salary for his duties as agent; but if the project produced a profit, he would share equally in it with his two partners.[26]

James genuinely felt that such a plan would benefit the freedmen. He maintained that in the aftermath of the Civil War, similar labor schemes established throughout the South were probably the only realistic means by which former slaves might gain a substantial economic foothold—especially since the Johnson administration's position was apparently to discontinue the bureau and leave the freedmen to their own resources and at the mercy of unsympathetic whites.[27]

Backed by his experience at the Trent River settlement and in the bureau's Eastern District, James launched the Pitt County venture with hopeful anticipation of establishing a successful cotton plantation. He assumed his duties as supervisor of the farms on Christmas Day, 1865, and was accompanied to his residence at Avon plantation by his wife and child. The combined plantations under his care consisted of 1,200 acres of land, on which 200 freedmen were employed and between 400 and 500 resided.

James had no written contracts with his laborers, but he agreed orally to pay at a rate ranging from $5.00 plus rations per month for boy workers to $15.00 plus rations for adult males. He also maintained a plantation store from which he sold clothing under the same arrangement as in New Bern and James City. His farms produced a number of crops in addition to cotton. He permitted the laborers to keep their own gardens and raise hogs and chickens for their own consumption. He gave the

---

[26] *New York Times*, July 29, 1866; Colonel Eliphalet Whittlesey to Major General John B. Steedman, April 28, 1866, Letters Sent, Freedmen's Bureau Records, RG 105.

[27] Captain Horace James to the Secretaries of the American Missionary Association, October 20, 1865, AMA Archives, North Carolina Letters.

freedmen Saturday afternoons and Sundays off, delivering sermons to them on the Sabbath.[28]

James established a school for freedmen on the two plantations; it was operated by two teachers from the American Missionary Association, Kate A. Means and Harriet S. Billings. The teachers held both day and evening classes and taught children and adults. They also conducted a Sunday school. The former slaves placed great stock in being able to attend school, and when it opened its doors in January, 1866, the Yankee Hall school alone had 103 students who were "trying hard to learn to be something."[29]

This engraving appeared in *Harper's Weekly* in 1868 above the caption "James's Plantation School, North Carolina." The precise location of this school is not given, but it is possibly one of the schools established in 1866 by Horace James at the Avon and Yankee Hall plantations in Pitt County. From "The Freedmen's Schools," *Harper's Weekly*, XII (October 3, 1868), p. 637.

The plantations operated for several months amid an air of optimism among the superintendent, the missionaries, and the laborers. But the bright promise of the scheme was soon dulled by an incident that resulted in the death of one of the freedmen and the subsequent military trial of James.

---

[28] Undated manuscript by Horace James, AMA Archives, North Carolina Letters; McFeely, *Yankee Stepfather*, 251; *Trial of Rev. Horace James, before a special military commission, convened by direction of Andrew Johnson, President of the United States in September, 1866*, 6. A printed transcript of the trial, which was held in Raleigh, is in the North Carolina Collection, University of North Carolina Library, Chapel Hill (it will hereinafter be cited as *Trial of Rev. Horace James, September, 1866*); *Freedmen's Journal* (New York), September, 1866; D. A. Bacon to E. P. Smith, August 5, 1867, AMA Archives, North Carolina Letters.

[29] Horace James to "My dear Bro[ther]," January 19, 1866, AMA Archives, North Carolina Letters.

On March 10, 1866, three black laborers from Yankee Hall broke into one of the plantation's storerooms. They stole some clothing but were soon apprehended by David Boyden, the white overseer of the farm. Boyden took the culprits to James for disciplining. Two of the men were admonished for their actions and released. But the third, Alsbury Keel, was sentenced by James to dig ditches on the Avon plantation. According to the subsequent testimony of two freedmen, Keel had been in trouble before. James later argued that he was too far from local law enforcement and military authorities to turn Keel over to them. Instead, he instructed the Avon overseer, Joseph B. Johnson, to assign Keel to the supervision of another freedman, John Izzy, and to give Izzy a revolver with which to guard Keel. After approximately an hour and a half of ditching, Keel fled from Izzy, who did not attempt to restrain him, and hid in a swamp near the Tar River, which divided the two plantations. The following evening Lamb Grimes, black foreman at Yankee Hall, and two other laborers who were fishing discovered Keel crossing the river. Grimes informed overseer Boyden, who went to the riverbank and found Keel there. Upon seeing Boyden, the fugitive attempted to escape by swimming. According to the testimony of Grimes, Boyden repeatedly ordered Keel to halt and then fired at him with a revolver. Having shot once, Boyden then ordered Keel to surrender; unheeded, Boyden fired a second time, evidently killing Keel.[30]

James immediately reported the incident to Major General F. A. Seely, assistant commissioner of the Eastern District of the Freedmen's Bureau, who had earlier replaced James in the position. Seely informed his superior, Whittlesey, of the incident and asked what legal action should be taken. On March 15, 1866, Whittlesey replied: "I believe the law treats such cases of homicide as justifiable and have referred Capt. James to the recent statute in this state on the subject. As the affair seems to have occurred at night, and as the body of the negro has not [yet] been discovered it does not appear certain that the shot took effect, no further action in the case seems to be called for."[31]

Apparently the law to which Whittlesey referred was a North Carolina statute entitled "An Act to Outlaw Felons Who Flee from Justice." The law, ratified March 1, 1866, gave citizens legal authority to shoot felons who refused to surrender. It applied, however, only to those felons who had been proclaimed outlaws by the courts, which was not

---

[30] *Trial of Rev. Horace James, September, 1866*, 6-10.
[31] *Trial of Rev. Horace James, September, 1866*, 24; Lieutenant Fred H. Beecher to Major General O. O. Howard, March 15, 1866, Endorsements Sent, Freedmen's Bureau Records, RG 105.

the case with Keel. Despite Whittlesey's opinion, James submitted a full report of the incident; and on March 28, 1866, the report received the endorsement of bureau headquarters in Raleigh.[32] In May military authorities arrested James. The charges brought against him alleged that he had pursued Keel and ordered Boyden to shoot him, and later had attempted to cover up the incident. He was alleged also to be operating the Pitt County plantations for his own benefit and "thereby becoming interested, for his own profit and involvement, in the labor of the said freedmen, in derrogation of his official duty as [a bureau] agent."[33]

The charges brought against James resulted in large measure from the activities of Generals James Scott Fullerton and John B. Steedman, who were appointed by President Andrew Johnson "to investigate the [Freedmen's] Bureau and to expose the members who reportedly mistreated Negroes in order to convince the nation that there were justifiable reasons for terminating the agency." The shooting incident at Yankee Hall occurred while Fullerton and Steedman were investigating Freedmen's Bureau affairs in North Carolina, and they seized upon the incident as a means of discrediting the bureau in the state.[34] Coupled with a similar, simultaneous investigation at James City (which will be discussed), it did succeed in casting an aura of suspicion over the bureau's activities in the state.

A military commission tried James in Raleigh in September, 1866. No evidence was produced to support the allegation that James told Boyden to shoot the fugitive Alsbury Keel, and James was proven not to have been present when the shooting occurred. Moreover, John Izzy, the laborer assigned to guard Keel at Avon, testified that James gave him specific instructions not to shoot Keel but to use the revolver only to intimidate him. Izzy claimed that overseer Joseph B. Johnson was the only man who said, "if this boy tries to get away from you, you shoot him."

As a refutation of the charge that James deliberately and systematically mistreated the freedmen, the black laborers subpoenaed by the court testified that he provided rations, medicine, doctor's care, land for gardens and livestock, and free schools and always paid them on time each month. They insisted that they were better off working for him than for their former masters.

John Izzy also testified that William Grimes had threatened to paddle slaves who begged for meat to supplement their meager rations, whereas James gave adequate rations as well as pay. Furthermore, Izzy

---

[32] *Public Laws of North Carolina, 1866*, c. 62, s. 1.
[33] *Trial of Rev. Horace James, September, 1866*, 3.
[34] McFeely, *Yankee Stepfather*, 246-247, 252.

pointed out that the missionary teachers had taught him to read and write—even giving him a gilt-edged Bible as a reward for being "the one who learned the fastest." [35] The American Missionary Association teachers verified the freedmen's opinion of James, as did the native white overseers. "He is certainly a true and warm friend to the colored people," wrote Harriet S. Billings. "He surely has the love of those on his plantations." [36]

In answer to the charge that James was involved in a conflict of interest in the operation of the plantations, Major Seely testified that James was a civilian and accepted no pay from the government. He further testified that James had not approached him about being a bureau agent but that he had asked the minister to accept the responsibilities in addition to his plantation interests, stressing that Pitt County had no bureau agent and that James's experience might prove valuable. [37] The American Missionary Association had likewise beseeched James to continue to assist the organization in a consulting capacity if he would not accept an offer to become association secretary. On December 5, 1865, James had written an official of the American Missionary Association declining the secretaryship and informing him that

I have resigned my army office, and expect to be mustered out this month, but shall continue to be a civilian agent of the Bureau in a rural district where I can help to settle the labor question which is now so uncertain and dubious a condition, and supervise in connection with it certain large agricultural matters in which I shall have a personal interest. This will require me to spend most of my time in N. Carolina, but will leave me sufficient time to aid your society by effort and correspondence in your work in N.C. This I will do without compensation, nor shall I have any compensation as an agent of the Bureau. But if you should want me to make any journeys or inspection tours on your business, I shall permit you to pay my travelling expenses. [38]

No evidence was produced at the trial to show that James had operated the stores on the Pitt County plantations for his own profit.

The court acquitted James of all the charges against him. James's final statement to the court indicates that he was embittered and disillusioned for having been tried by the government he had served so long and faithfully. Whittlesey was also tried for failing to investigate Keel's

---

[35] *Trial of Rev. Horace James, September, 1866,* 16-18.
[36] Harriet S. Billings to Samuel Hunt, May 3, 1866, AMA Archives, North Carolina Letters.
[37] *Trial of Rev. Horace James, September, 1866,* 22-24.
[38] Captain Horace James to Rev. Mr. Strieby, December 5, 1865, AMA Archives, North Carolina Letters.

death and for exploiting the freedmen. He too was acquitted. There was no trial of the white overseer accused of shooting Keel. General Howard, under pressure from the Johnson government to force Whittlesey to resign, transferred him back to his own staff in Washington, D.C. The Pitt County plantations continued for a short time; but a failure of the cotton crop resulted in a dissolution of the enterprise, and the property reverted to its original owner in January, 1867.[39]

James returned to Massachusetts in that year and took charge of a parish in Lowell, serving also as associate editor of the *Congregationalist*. He then traveled abroad. While visiting Palestine he contracted a severe cold, resulting in consumption and ultimately his death in Worcester, Massachusetts, on June 9, 1875.[40]

Horace James's service to North Carolina blacks had been considerable. James had originally committed himself to the propagation of the gospel as a Congregational minister but in a burst of patriotism answered Lincoln's call to save the Union. Although a vocal opponent of slavery, he had at first hoped for its gradual eradication. But as a result of his war experience he came to believe in the immediate abolition of the South's social blight, which in his view retarded the nation's moral and economic growth. Despite his idealistic and sincere devotion to the freedmen, James was no radical innovator. He felt that blacks were biologically and intellectually inferior and therefore could never achieve full social equality with whites. He endorsed the prevailing nineteenth-century American economic theory of laissez faire and insisted that the federal government's role in the South should last only long enough to provide former slaves with a chance for a better life through education and hard work. Nevertheless, James's moderate views on economic and social change did not tarnish his idealistic hope for a better world for blacks in the South—a hope that lived on at a rickety outpost on the Trent River near New Bern.

---

[39] *Trial of Rev. Horace James, September, 1866*, 26-29; McFeely, *Yankee Stepfather*, 253; D. A. Bacon to E. P. Smith, August 5, December 3, 1867, AMA Archives, North Carolina Letters.

[40] Mary L. Thornton, "The Promised Land on the Trent," *News and Observer*, March 19, 1961; *Evening Gazette*, June 10, 1875.

III. THE TRENT RIVER SETTLEMENT, 1863-1869

When the Trent River camp was first established in 1863 it had a crude appearance. An early visitor to the camp, H. S. Beals of the American Missionary Association, recorded his observations:

At 11 o'clock A.M. I crossed to the South Bank of the Trent to a contraband camp, where I spent a day of thrilling interest. There are about twelve hundred men, women, & children, in the camp, gathered from inland portions of the state, Goldsborough, and elsewhere. Near the entrance of the village, at the door of a hut under a piece of canvas, I found a man preaching to a few of his neighbors, and nearby two hundred colored soldiers. The preacher had no church connection, had preached seven years along the borders of the dismal swamp, called himself a prophet, had other strange, wild ideas. I talked to them, by permission nearly half an hour. They paid good attention appearing to feel, that their hope rested in their own efforts, mainly for freedom and justice.

Beals returned the following day and conversed freely with the inhabitants about conditions in the camp. He found that there were about 600 children with no regular or Sabbath school and that one literate old black man was teaching a few of them. He observed sixty or seventy children running about the village with no clothing except long shirts made from sails, bags, or sacks. He felt that the camp needed 600 textbooks, a teacher, and a "good pastor to mould, by clear exhibitions of divine truth their crude faith, and soften & soothe their exciting mode of worship."[1]

Despite the crude beginnings and the demands of war, the camp had undergone considerable improvement by 1865. A few months after the close of the war Horace James marveled at the progress the freedmen had made in establishing a permanent and self-supporting settlement. "It was started," he declared,

as a temporary camp, in which to place colored fugitives and give them food and protection, while the country was disturbed by war. At one time nearly 2500 people were fed in that camp, now there are not 300 all total, who receive assistance. Many of the people are laying up property, own mules, horses and carts, or are keeping little shops, or running some mechanical trade. They [show] no disposition to move back into the country, but being well able to support themselves here. They choose this method of gaining a livelihood. In fact, the village is now self-supporting. The income received from it in the month of August was $935. The expenses of it were several hundred dollars less. There seems therefore to be no prospect of this village being abandoned and its people scattered out into the country unless it is done by force.[2]

---

[1] H. S. Beals to S. S. Jocelyn, August 18, 1863, AMA Archives, North Carolina Letters.

[2] Captain Horace James to Lieutenant Fred H. Beecher, September 20, 1865, Letters Received, Freedmen's Bureau Records, RG 105.

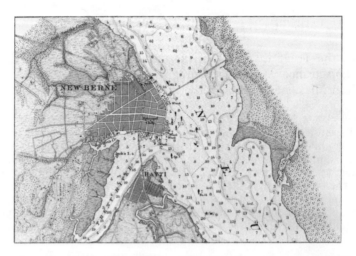

Shown above is a portion of an 1867 map delineating the area surrounding New Bern. The Trent River settlement, lying south of New Bern on the opposite side of the Trent River, is shown as "Hayti," a general geographic term commonly used in maps of the era to denote a predominantly black area. From "U.S. Coast Survey, Benjamin Peirce, Superintendent. Part of New Berne, North Carolina" (1867), Map Collection, State Archives.

James emphasized that the Trent River settlement had become an important suburb of New Bern; and he estimated in 1865 that the lots there, which could have been worth no more than $10.00 before the war, would then sell for $200. He insisted that the camp was "well ordered, great, quiet, healthy and better regulated than the city proper" and that the only improvement needed was the replacing of the many temporary shanties with more permanent buildings. This could be done, he wrote, if the federal government would purchase the land and resell lots to the freedmen. Such action would "induce them [the freedmen] to put permanent improvements on them" because they would be certain of improving property that was legally theirs. He suggested that the bureau be authorized to purchase the land "of the old owners, from such funds as we command," and turn it over to the freedmen.

Many of the camp's residents had already built more substantial structures. "To show what these improvements are worth," James declared, "I will state, that one little building erected for a shop sold yesterday for $55. This settlement of colored people is really a valuable part of the City of New Berne and should no longer be a mere squatter upon the lands of other parties." Colonel Whittlesey approved of James's suggestion to purchase the land if he could and advised him that if it

44

could not be bought, he should "obtain a lease for it as long as possible." [3]

Although James wanted to see the Trent River camp made a permanent settlement for blacks, he did not want its population to grow. Instead, he attempted to keep as many freedmen as possible on the farms and plantations in eastern North Carolina and encouraged those in the New Bern area who could safely do so to return to the countryside. He realized that a flood of more blacks to camps such as James City would be self-defeating because not all could find work and the bureau would be hard pressed to provide for them. The result would probably be an increase in vagrancy and disease. One New Bern newspaper noted and applauded James's efforts to check vagrancy when it declared:

We do not propose to lash any particular race, for this failing of which we complain has attacked the white race to an alarming extent. There are hundreds of whites who have not a dollar in the world, who lag around the public places of our city without any visible or invisible means of support. They do not even earn the bread they eat, but manage to eke out a scanty living.

We have been informed . . . that Capt. James has recently sent away into the country, to seek employment, several thousands of colored people, who are able to labor in the corn fields—couldn't the Captain send some white ones too? We are glad to see this movement as it indicates a fixed purpose to encourage habits of industry, while they at the same time are laboring for the elevation of the race. Those who have left to seek employment have been very successful, and are now earning their own livelihood like men.[4]

Colonel Whittlesey reported to General Howard that there were more white refugee vagrants in North Carolina towns than blacks because most blacks were in camps like James City or were still on the farms and plantations.[5]

After James moved to Pitt County, his successors continued the effort to settle the James City freedmen in the countryside. Like James, they were willing to cooperate with and assist native whites who would treat the freedmen fairly. In one joint venture near James City, seven miles from New Bern near the boundary line between Craven and Jones counties, the bureau participated in an ambitious plantation enterprise. It was known as the Lyon Pasture plantation and was managed by Isaac A. Brooks, a local white farmer who rented the land from a Goldsboro

---

[3] Colonel Eliphalet Whittlesey to Major General O. O. Howard, First Quarterly Report, 1865, and Whittlesey to Captain Horace James, September 25, 1865, Letters Sent, Freedmen's Bureau Records, RG 105; James to Lieutenant Fred H. Beecher, September 20, 1865, Letters Received, Freedmen's Bureau Records, RG 105.

[4] *Daily North Carolina Times* (New Bern), July 21, 1865, hereinafter cited as *Daily North Carolina Times*.

[5] Colonel Eliphalet Whittlesey to Major General O. O. Howard, First Quarterly Report, 1865, Letters Sent, Freedmen's Bureau Records, RG 105.

Two views of the Trent River settlement, 1866. Shown at top is a railroad bridge that spanned the Trent River and linked the settlement with New Bern; at bottom is a group of freedmen standing near their rude dwellings. These engravings, as well as the cover illustration, were sketched by Theodore R. Davis and reproduced in *Harper's Weekly*, X (June 9, 1866), p. 361.

lawyer named Isler. Under the agreement between Brooks and the bureau, the farm was to provide employment for a number of destitute freedmen and also orphans of former slaves. The bureau furnished all the laborers and their rations and constructed barracks in which to house the plantation's workers and orphans. Brooks provided the tools, feed, seed, firewood, transportation to work, and the sites for the barracks. He and the laborers divided equally the products of the farm, of which the chief crops were cotton and corn. The bureau constructed seven buildings on the property, including two barracks, a corncrib, a storehouse, and a house for the agent of the bureau. The number of destitutes and orphans on the plantation varied from twenty-five to fifty. Crop failures and quarrels with the owner of the land eventually led to the dissolution of the enterprise. In February, 1867, the bureau abandoned the plantation and sold its buildings at public auction.[6]

Under the direction of James the Trent River settlement got off to a good start and began making a contribution to the economy of New Bern. In September the camp contained 790 "negro cabins," 12 small

---

[6] Isaac A. Brooks to Brevet Major J. J. Van Horne, [?] 1866, Letters Received, Records of the United States Army Continental Commands, 1821-1920, Department of North Carolina, Record Group 393, Letter Book 174/375, p. 25, National Archives, Washington, D.C., hereinafter cited as Letters Received or Letters Sent, U.S. Army Continental Command, Department of North Carolina, RG 393; Report from the Eastern District, October 30, 1866, Reports of Operations (Annual), Freedmen's Bureau Records, RG 105; Endorsement of March 16, 1867, Endorsements Sent, Freedmen's Bureau Records, RG 105.

stores, 5 churches, and 7 government buildings that included 2 office buildings, a market house, and a large government store. The bureau assigned to the black dwellings an average value of not less than $30.00 each.[7]

Most of the families farmed the bureau's land located to the south and adjacent to the village. A large part of this land belonged to the heirs of Peter G. Evans, whose holdings south of the Trent River included thousands of acres in addition to the portion on which the camp stood. The farmers of James City may have tilled as many as 500 acres at the outset of Reconstruction, but the acreage that came under the plow later declined. The largest tract assigned to any person or family consisted of 4 acres of enclosed land and 12 acres of open land.[8] Much of the produce of James City farmland found a market in New Bern. Many of the camp residents worked in New Bern as laborers and at other jobs. Produce sellers and tradesmen traveled back and forth across the Trent River bridge, which the contrabands had constructed during the war. "This bridge," declared the New Bern *Daily North Carolina Times* in June, 1865, "which connects New Bern with that portion of the outer world beyond the Trent is a fine institution. Besides serving the purpose of a railroad and wagon thoroughfare, it connects Hayti [James City] with the continent, and furnishes an easy and pleasant means of communication between the races. We counted eleven six-horse teams and wagons crossing at one time yesterday, and still there was room for eight or ten more."[9]

Immediately after the war James set forth rules and regulations governing commerce and conduct in the settlement, and on July 15, 1865, he announced that all residents "engaged in trade, whether keeping store, or selling commodities upon the streets, will be required to pay a tax for the support of the settlement." The tax for keeping a shop was $5.00 per month; for selling at a stand or on the street, $2.00 per month. No tax was levied on the sale of produce from local gardens. James mandated that those who came to the camp by boat or crossed the bridge to trade with the James City residents "will be liable to taxation at the same rates as in New Bern." These taxes made the settlement largely self-

---

[7] Report of Captain Horace James for the Eastern District for the Quarter ending September 30, 1865, Freedmen's Bureau Records, RG 105.

[8] Colonel Eliphalet Whittlesey to Brigadier General J. A. Campbell, May 7, 1866, Letters Sent, Freedmen's Bureau Records, RG 105; Monthly Reports of Abandoned and Confiscated Lands, 1865, Freedmen's Bureau Records, RG 105; Roberta Sue Alexander, "North Carolina Faces the Freedmen: Race Relations in North Carolina during Presidential Reconstruction" (unpublished doctoral dissertation, University of Chicago, 1974), 434-435, hereinafter cited as Alexander, "North Carolina Faces the Freedmen."

[9] *Daily North Carolina Times*, June 21, 1865.

supporting.[10] From tax revenues the inhabitants paid the superintendent of the camp, his assistant, a clerk, 6 nurses, and 15 mechanics and laborers. They also paid for repairs to the public buildings. Aside from rations and medical supplies, no governmental aid went toward the support of the residents of James City. In October, 1865, General Whittlesey reported that out of about 3,000 freedmen in the camp, all but about 10 percent were self-supporting. At that time only 169 women, 275 children, and 20 men (10 of whom were in the hospital) were receiving aid from the government. During the entire Reconstruction period only a small fraction of the total population of the Trent River settlement, primarily women and children, received government aid. (See Appendix, Table 5.)

The bureau superintendent in charge of the camp established law and order and prescribed the punishment for violations. Close observance of the Sabbath was required, and the consumption of alcohol was strictly forbidden while James remained subassistant commissioner for the Eastern District.[11]

The task of educating the former slaves rested with northern philanthropic organizations. Schools were first established when the camp was created in 1863. The first one was the Russell School, commissioned by the Boston Educational Society and the American Missionary Association in September, 1863. In February, 1864, the teacher in charge, Miss Sarah M. Pearson, reported that 280 pupils were enrolled, 200 of whom constituted the largest number present at any session. She taught spelling, reading, writing, geography, arithmetic, and singing.[12]

During the war the teachers at the camp exhibited a special courage in remaining there, for it was frequently threatened by bombardment when Confederate forces attempted and failed to recapture New Bern. On one such occasion in February, 1864, Miss Pearson recorded that she had commenced classes with 200 pupils when "towards noon it became

---

[10] Order of Captain Horace James, July 15, 1865, as reported in the *New Berne Daily Times*, May 7, 1866; Colonel Eliphalet Whittlesey to Major General O. O. Howard, First Quarterly Report, 1865, Letters Sent, Freedmen's Bureau Records, RG 105; Whittlesey to Brigadier General J. A. Campbell, May 7, 1866, Letters Sent, Freedmen's Bureau Records, RG 105; Captain Horace James to Lieutenant Fred H. Beecher, September 20, 1865, Registered Letters Received, Freedmen's Bureau Records, RG 105.

[11] Statistical Reports of Operations for the Month Ending October 13, 1865, Freedmen's Bureau Records, RG 105; Miscellaneous Ration Reports, November-December, 1866, Freedmen's Bureau Records, RG 105; Report of Rations Issued and Related Records, 1865-1868, Freedmen's Bureau Records, RG 105.

[12] Monthly Report of a Colored School Taught by Sarah M. Pearson in New Berne for the Month of February, 1864 and Monthly Report of a Colored School Taught by Sarah M. Pearson in New Berne for the Month of June, 1864, AMA Archives, North Carolina Letters.

apparent we could no longer go on with the exercises owing to the excitement growing out of the continuous firing of cannons from the neighboring forts." In April, 1864, she wrote: "the school has again been disturbed through fear of rebel invasion, something of a panic existed for a few days, and my whole number has been less than it was during the last month. Many of the pupils expressing great fear as to the result of their being found in school, should the enemy appear, they are now, in a measure reassured. These various interruptions . . . prevent my carrying my plans to a successful issue."[13]

Miss Pearson had two assistants to aid her in teaching the freedmen, and all three teachers were generally impressed with the children's dedication to education. "Their earnestness of manner together with their simple faith is touching to witness," one teacher observed. Miss Susan A. Hosmer, one of the assistant teachers, was particularly moved by a pupil who "wished we could see the marks of the lash upon her back. They were an inch wide."[14]

In addition to the threat posed by possible Confederate attack, Miss Pearson faced other problems in keeping some of her black students in class. Cold weather and frequent repairs to the school building sometimes required that classes be suspended. At other times the building had to be used as a hospital during epidemics or to treat wounded soldiers. "Sickness," wrote Miss Hosmer in June, 1864, is "still prevalent in Camp, many have died, . . . our school room was taken for a hospital for a few days, one woman died in the Recitation room, a young boy after he was removed also died, it seems strange to enter those rooms & teach after death has been there." Many of the scholars departed the school upon finding employment, and still others had their government rations cut off and were forced to leave and find work in order to eat.[15]

In addition to teaching her regular students, Miss Pearson conducted classes after hours for a number of black soldiers and adults who worked during the day. Miss Pearson evidently departed James City sometime in 1865, but her school was continued by other northern teachers, some of whom lived in New Bern and were transported to the camp by military ambulance. The number of students continued to decline as the realities of Reconstruction forced many of the youths from the classroom into the labor force. Miss Mary E. Jones, a teacher,

---

[13] Monthly Report of a Colored School Taught by Sarah M. Pearson in New Berne for the Month of April, 1864, AMA Archives, North Carolina Letters.

[14] Reverend W. J. Biggs to George Whipple, February 12, 1864, and Susan A. Hosmer to Whipple, September 11, 1863, AMA Archives, North Carolina Letters.

[15] Susan A. Hosmer to George Whipple, June 10, 1864, and Monthly Report of Sarah M. Pearson for May, 1865, AMA Archives, North Carolina Letters.

49

reported in August, 1865, that she had a total of 90 pupils, of whom 75 might be present at one session; however, 81 of these students could read and spell. She pointed out that those who attended regularly had become good readers, could write "sufficiently well to pen me a letter," and knew some arithmetic and geography. Those who had the advantage of regular attendance and instruction surprised their teachers and even northern missionary officials who visited the camp, some of whom took a patronizing view of what they considered the limited capacity of blacks. Miss Jones reported one such clear indication of patronization:

Some gentlemen from Boston called one day, who thought at first the students were giving answers to a set of questions learned with little reference to their meaning. They inquired if such was not the case. The scholars resented the idea, alluding to it after they left. They affirmed that they understood it all, for, says one "t'would be our own fault if we did not, you had splained it enough." [16]

So long as the Federal military remained in the New Bern area, James City had no difficulty in obtaining teachers. In fact, more teachers came to the vicinity from the North than could be placed. "The Boston and N. York Freedmen's Societies," James wrote in October, 1865, "have sent so many teachers to New Bern that there seems to be no room for any more at present. They are very much crowded. We have but one small house for them on this side of the river, while several live over in the Trent River Settlement." [17] The northern teachers did not conduct classes at the camp during the summer months but instead returned to their homes. The subassistant commissioner for the Eastern District testified to the accomplishments of these teachers when, following their departure in the summer of 1867, he remarked that "the effects of their labors are visible in many forms, colored men buying and reading the newspapers, their children reading books."

The freedmen did not, however, rely solely upon white teachers. In the summer of 1867 they hired a black man named Morris to teach classes. A black woman, Rachel Thomas, having been a bright student of the missionaries, soon became knowledgeable enough to establish a school at the camp. The American Freedmen's Union Commission of New York employed her as a teacher and paid her a salary of $20.00 per month. For various periods of time during Reconstruction she was the only teacher in James City. [18]

---

[16] *National Freedmen* (New York), August 15, 1865.

[17] Captain Horace James to S. S. Ashley, October 30, 1865, AMA Archives, North Carolina Letters.

[18] Annual Report of the Sub-Assistant Commissioner of Sub-District 3, Lieutenant Colonel Stephen Moore, September 25, 1867, Freedmen's Bureau Records, RG 105.

The Mount Shiloh First Baptist Church, founded in 1866, has long been one of James City's most important institutions. This building, erected in 1924, presently serves the Mount Shiloh congregation. Photograph by Walton Haywood; from the files of the Division of Archives and History.

Like the missionary schools, churches were an important influence in the lives of the camp residents. At least four congregations, consisting of Baptist or A.M.E. Zion worshippers, existed in the community during the half decade following the Civil War, and their pastors were community leaders. Perhaps the most influential and most attended church was the Mount Shiloh First Baptist Church, founded in 1866.[19]

During the early phases of Reconstruction the residents of James City began working toward the acquisition of political rights. In the summer of 1865 many of them attended a convention of blacks that assembled in New Bern to demand legal equality and the right to vote. The convention was led by Abraham H. Galloway, a northern black, former Union soldier, and radical advocate of equal rights for his race. Delegates resolved that they should make "earnest efforts by education, virtue, industry, and economy to qualify ourselves for the higher stations of life. . . ." The members also insisted that the right to vote was their "*blood bought right,*" essential for survival in a white-dominated society. They then elected delegates to a statewide convention of blacks to be held in Raleigh as a means of influencing the Reconstruction con-

---

[19] Alexander, "North Carolina Faces the Freedmen," 434-435; author's interview with James C. Delemar, James City, March 24, 1980 (notes on interview in possession of author), hereinafter cited as Delemar interview, March 24, 1980.

vention of whites then meeting in the capital for the purpose of declaring slavery abolished, repudiating the state war debt, and providing for the election of governor, legislators, and representatives in Congress. President Andrew Johnson's moderate plan of reconstruction required these actions before North Carolina could be readmitted to the Union.[20]

The white inhabitants of New Bern took a dim view of this political activity on the part of James City blacks, and in September, 1865, the *New Berne Daily Times* declared that the inhabitants of the Trent River camp should give up such ideas and concentrate on improving their economic condition. "Already," the editor declared,

we have been informed of a sad condition of want among those colonized on the other side of Trent River. Every day we see or hear of destitute negroes from "slabtown," begging food; and it does not require the spirit of prophecy to foretell that much suffering must exist in that settlement the approaching winter.

The reason through which he can live in comparative comfort and ease will close in a few days—nay is now over—and the earth will no longer yield him of her bounty. The cool winds will whistle about his ears soon; and the icy breath of winter will demand more fuel and raiment.

Would it not be wisdom, then, to drop for a season the aspirations for political privileges.[21]

In spite of that advice, James City blacks dispatched Joseph Green, an A.M.E. Zion minister and a carpenter, as a delegate to the convention of blacks that assembled in Raleigh on September 29, 1865. The New Bern delegation, of which Green was a member, was the largest one at the Raleigh meeting. Influenced by the New Bern contingent, the convention appealed for black suffrage and other rights. But efforts to influence the white Reconstruction convention failed: the white delegates paid no attention to the appeal for black suffrage.[22]

Yet the issue did not rest there. The United States Congress refused to seat North Carolina's newly elected representatives and in 1867 substituted its own plan of reconstruction for that of President Johnson. The new plan took shape with the passage of the Reconstruction Acts of March, 1867, which divided the South into five military districts. North and South Carolina were placed in the Second District. Following the imposition of military authority to protect blacks and Unionists, the Republican party was formed in North Carolina. The residents of James City, like virtually all freedmen in the state, supported the new party

---

[20] Alexander, "North Carolina Faces the Freedmen," 64-66.
[21] *New Berne Daily Times*, September 28, 1865.
[22] Alexander, "North Carolina Faces the Freedmen," 64-66, 71-74, 78.

because it had ended slavery and had secured various legal and political rights for members of their race.[23]

Under the congressional plan, blacks in North Carolina were given the right to vote for or against the calling of a convention to draft a new state constitution. During the autumn of 1867 elections were held to decide this matter. The number of blacks in Craven County (including those in James City) who registered to vote in this election outnumbered the county's registered whites by 3,108 to 1,509. Craven County whites who had joined the new Conservative party (a coalition of prewar Democrats and former Whigs) generally opposed the drafting of a new constitution and hoped to discredit the election by refusing to register or vote. In the surrounding counties of Carteret, Beaufort, Hyde, Jones, Onslow, and Pitt the number of whites registered to vote exceeded the number of registered blacks.[24] Voters in these counties joined with those throughout the state in approving the constitutional convention, which met early in 1868.

The new state constitution, which was ratified in a separate election, accorded to blacks certain voting and legal rights. Many newly enfranchised blacks, including those in James City, thereupon joined with whites and elected new state and county officers and representatives in Congress. The newly elected state legislature ratified the Fourteenth Amendment to the United States Constitution, which extended federal protection to the civil rights of blacks. Following the amendment's ratification and the election of United States senators by the legislature in July, North Carolina was readmitted to the Union.[25]

During the time the black citizens of James City made their first venture into politics, the Ku Klux Klan became active in the state. The Klan was formed primarily to aid the Conservative party in political contests with Republicans in portions of the South. Its goal was to keep blacks from participating in Reconstruction politics by intimidating them with threats and violence. The Klan also labored to prevent blacks from achieving social equality with whites. In North Carolina these hooded or

---

[23] Hugh Talmage Lefler and Albert Ray Newsome, *North Carolina: The History of a Southern State* (Chapel Hill: University of North Carolina Press, Third Edition, 1973), 486-487, hereinafter cited as Lefler and Newsome, *North Carolina*; Richard L. Zuber, *North Carolina during Reconstruction* (Raleigh: Department of Cultural Resources, Division of Archives and History, second printing, 1975), 12-13, hereinafter cited as Zuber, *North Carolina during Reconstruction*.

[24] Zuber, *North Carolina during Reconstruction*, 13-14; Major J. J. Van Horne to the Acting Assistant Adjutant General for the Department of the South, October 1, 1867, Letters Sent, U.S. Army Continental Command, Department of North Carolina, RG 393, Letter Book 174/375, p. 22.

[25] Lefler and Newsome, *North Carolina*, 487-491; *New York Times*, April 9, 1888.

masked night riders were most active in the state's piedmont counties, where the black population was relatively small. There the Klan engaged in acts of violence, dispensing whippings and sometimes even resorting to murder. Such tactics intimidated many blacks and white Unionists and discouraged them from engaging in political activity. But because both James City and Craven County had sizable populations of freedmen who could retaliate against Klan attack, local blacks did not fall prey to the activities of this violent arm of the Conservative party. As a result of a federal campaign launched in 1871 to suppress the Klan, the terrorist organization disappeared from North Carolina the following year and did not reappear there until the 1920s (in a somewhat different form). The people of James City continued to exercise the right to vote, casting their ballots mainly for Republicans and black candidates during the remainder of the nineteenth century.[26]

Although the James City experiment had enjoyed relative success at the outset of Reconstruction, events that transpired in Washington, D.C., in 1866 had a detrimental effect on the future progress of the settlement. These events resulted from actions taken by President Andrew Johnson to bring to a close the operations of the Freedmen's Bureau, the driving force behind the James City colony. The original Freedmen's Bureau bill (1865) had specified that the agency was to exist for only one year, and Johnson opposed extension of the bureau's operations beyond that time limit.[27] In response, bureau officials throughout the South began to scale down the operations of the agency by breaking up settlements of freedmen, decreasing rations and other forms of aid, and restoring land to its original white owners.

In April, 1866, Colonel Whittlesey reported from North Carolina that "the number of destitute freedmen dependent upon the government has been gradually reduced, and it is hoped that by the end of another quarter, the necessity of gratuitous issue of rations and clothing will have ceased entirely." Whittlesey further reported that, in response to the president's orders concerning the bureau, he had advised the freedmen of Roanoke Island and James City that all bureau aid might be cut off and the inhabitants dispersed as early as May 1.[28]

26 Zuber, *North Carolina during Reconstruction*, 26-28, 46-47; Otto H. Olsen, "The Ku Klux Klan: A Study in Reconstruction Politics and Propaganda," *North Carolina Historical Review*, XXXIX (July, 1962), 340-362; Election Records and Returns, Craven County Miscellaneous Papers, Volumes C.R. 028.912.1 (1874-1908) and C.R. 028.912.2 (1878-1900) and Box C.R. 028.912.9 (1878-1890), State Archives, hereinafter cited as Craven County Election Records and Returns.

27 McKitrick, *Andrew Johnson and Reconstruction*, 286-287; Allen W. Trelease, *Reconstruction: The Great Experiment* (New York: Harper and Row, 1971), 55-56.

28 Colonel Eliphalet Whittlesey to Major General O. O. Howard, April 10, 1866, Letters Sent, Freedmen's Bureau Records, RG 105.

Johnson's policy toward the bureau was warmly greeted by eastern North Carolina whites. In April the *Daily Newbern Commercial* announced that it had heard the Trent River settlement would soon be broken up. "This is all right," declared the editor. "The feeding of the negroes at the common expense is nothing less than offering a premium for idleness. There is plenty of work to be had. It seems that a resolution has been come to by the Government authorities to force the negroes they are now feeding in idleness to work for their own living." [29] The *New Berne Daily Times* made these comments in favor of the disbandment of James City:

In the Trent River Settlement . . . there are about two thousand darkies, nearly all of whom are dependent upon the government. There are numbers of them who could work and support themselves but are indisposed to go back into the country where they could get work. In such cases there should be some plan devised to force them to work. It is a shame that the Government should be required to feed stout, healthy, negroes, whether male or female simply because they don't want to work. All such should be driven out of the camp and made to support themselves. [30]

But, as has been shown, most of the blacks in the camp were not dependent upon the government, and even those who were felt they had good reason not to return to working for their former masters or other whites on farms and plantations. Many of them doubted the honesty of white employers and viewed a return to the countryside as a reversion to the conditions of slavery from which they had fled. "In some cases," remarked one bureau official, "the negro still [has] a distrust for the word and obligation of the whites and is unwilling to receive their council [*sic*] or advice." [31] Having little fear of arrest by local civil authorities, who were appointees of state officials supported by President Johnson, some whites in the New Bern area made open attacks upon former slaves as well as other white North Carolinians who had remained loyal to the Union during the war. In October, 1866, the commanding officer at New Bern complained of lawless attacks by whites and remarked that he "could cite instances where men have been notified to move their property and threatened with the loss of it if they do not. The outrages are becoming more frequent occurrences and the civil authorities cannot and will not arrest the perpetrators." [32] At the Trent River camp the

[29] *Daily Newbern Commercial*, April 19, 1866.
[30] *New Bern Daily Times*, April 14, 1866.
[31] Colonel Eliphalet Whittlesey to Major General O. O. Howard, November 17, 1865, Letters Sent, Freedmen's Bureau Records, RG 105.
[32] Lieutenant H. E. Hagen to the Assistant Adjutant General of the Military Command of North Carolina, October 28, 1866, Letters Received, U.S. Army Continental Command, Department of North Carolina, RG 393, Letter Book 173/372, p. 105.

safety of numbers and the presence of Federal troops as a buffer against violent attacks from unsympathetic whites protected blacks during Presidential Reconstruction.

Encouraged by the support of white southerners, President Johnson continued his efforts to discredit the bureau; and his representatives in North Carolina, John B. Steedman and James S. Fullerton, seized on events at James City to achieve that end in the Tar Heel State. In March,

Union Generals James Scott Fullerton and John B. Steedman were appointed by President Andrew Johnson to investigate the activities of the Freedmen's Bureau in North Carolina. Shown above are the two generals conferring with the freedmen in a church at the Trent River settlement. Engraving, based on a sketch by Theodore R. Davis, from *Harper's Weekly*, X (June 9, 1866), p. 361.

1866, the camp was under the supervision of Edward S. Fitz, a former Massachusetts soldier and lay minister who had preached to a black congregation in New Bern during the Civil War. In that month an official of the American Missionary Association, Stephen W. Laidler, who had been sent to New Bern to establish a Congregational church, accused Fitz of mistreating the freedmen by unjust imprisonment and torture for violating camp rules. Laidler also claimed that the bureau agent was charging the freedmen excessive rent. The military authorities appointed a court of inquiry to investigate the charges, but before its work was completed some of the testimony was seized by General Steedman and published by the New York *Herald*, whose correspondent was accompanying the president's investigating commission. The *Herald* was a strong opponent of the bureau and a supporter of Johnson. The New York newspaper as well as the Conservative press of North Carolina seized upon the affair at the Trent River camp as "an example of the blatant ineptness of the Freedmen's Bureau." The investigation of Fitz occurred at about the same time that James and Whittlesey were involved in litigation over the Pitt County planting enterprise. Interestingly, in neither case did the federal investigators resort to the traditional claim that the bureau was wasting government funds and encouraging laziness by providing support for idle blacks. Extant records (obvious at least in the case of James City) indicate that this was not the case. Rather, the Johnson commission accused the bureau officers of mistreating and exploiting the former slaves and cited this as justification for terminating the bureau.[33]

When Fitz went before a court of inquiry, he was acquitted of most of the charges but was found guilty of mistreating some of the freedmen who violated camp rules—although not to the extent to which Laidler had accused him. The bureau ultimately dismissed Fitz from its service.

Fitz was not blameless, but both the secretary of the American Missionary Association and the chairman of the court of inquiry considered Laidler unstable and felt that he had brought charges against Fitz for personal reasons. The secretary found that Laidler had exaggerated his claims against Fitz and terminated Laidler's association with the society in July, 1866. The chairman of the court of inquiry also concluded that Laidler had attempted to influence witnesses and had claimed to have viewed incidents at James City that he obviously could not have seen.[34]

But the trial and dismissal of Fitz, as well as the trials and subsequent departure of James and Whittlesey, were used to reinforce President Johnson's opposition to continuation of the bureau. As a result of the adjutant general's orders, all rents at James City were discontinued and bureau aid decreased. Then, in July, 1866, the dispensing of all rations and clothing was terminated. At the same time, the bureau's sanitary inspector for the Eastern District visited the camp and reported that the "sanitary condition is not good" because the shanties were poorly built,

---

[33] S. F. Laidler to S. S. Jocelyn, March 30, 1866, and Laidler to the Secretaries of the American Missionary Association, April 20, 1866, AMA Archives, North Carolina Letters; U.S. Congress, Senate, *Report of the Secretary of War Communicating, In compliance with a resolution of the Senate of the 26th of May, a copy of the preliminary report, and also of the final report of the American Freedmen's Inquiry Commission*, Thirty-eighth Congress, First Session, 1863-1864, Senate Executive Document No. 53, p. 18; Semi-Monthly Report of the Condition of Freedmen and the Operations of the Freedmen's Bureau in the State of North Carolina, May 13, 1866, Reports of Statistical Operations, Freedmen's Bureau Records, RG 105; Colonel Eliphalet Whittlesey to Major General O. O. Howard, May 14, 1866, Letters Sent, Freedmen's Bureau Records, RG 105; *Southerner* (Tarboro), May 26, 1866.

[34] Linthicum, "The American Missionary Association and North Carolina Freedmen," 52-53.

overcrowded, and lacked proper sewage disposal and that a better well was needed.

Yet the inspector found at the camp some evidence to suggest that the activities of the bureau remained fundamentally benevolent and that the rents paid by the freedmen had been put to proper use. "I was gratified," he said,

in visiting the hospital of this settlement to see everything in and around the building, in so neat, clean, & creditable condition. Important improvements as to the comfort & efficiency of the establishment have been made since my last visit. The dining room, kitchen, & stewards room have been connected—a store room arranged—the whole building carefully whitewashed within & without, a good garden cultivated, places arranged for keeping fowls, a fishery established & a bakery in progress—thus providing for fresh & wholesome food for the patients, without any cost to the government.

The inspector further noted that the hospital had thirty-three patients and six attendants and employees and that he considered the bureau personnel to be attentive and diligent.[35]

In response to the inspector's report, Colonel W. W. Wiegel, sub-assistant commissioner for the Eastern District, ordered the demolition of all unoccupied buildings and also attempted "to induce the helpless and indigent Freedmen to remove to the Poor Farm [Lyon Pasture plantation] but without success."[36]

Notwithstanding President Johnson's efforts to disband the Freedmen's Bureau, Congress in July, 1866, passed, over his veto, a bill continuing the bureau for an indefinite period. But despite the passage of the new Freedmen's Bureau bill, the organization never regained the vitality that had enabled it to make its initially significant contributions to the welfare of former slaves. Along with similar events throughout the South, the investigation by the president's commission and the subsequent attacks on Whittlesey, James, and Fitz led the bureau to follow more closely the president's guidelines for assisting the freedmen and to eliminate the use of self-help programs in the form of rents or the consignment of abandoned lands. In addition, Johnson's policy of allowing southern state governments to manage their own affairs virtually prohibited the bureau from interfering in judicial cases involving former slaves.

In a number of cases in North Carolina in which freedmen were tried

---

[35] Report No. 8 on Trent River Settlement, July 12, 1866, Reports on Sanitary Conditions, Freedmen's Bureau Records, RG 105.

[36] Brevet Colonel W. W. Wiegel to Brevet Colonel C. A. Cilley, July 14, 1866, Reports on Sanitary Conditions, Freedmen's Bureau Records, RG 105.

in civil courts, freedmen did not receive a fair hearing and were unjustly punished. "I am satisfied that the negro has very little chance of getting his due before the Civil Courts of North Carolina at present," Colonel Whittlesey wrote to General Howard. Although the new criminal laws in North Carolina made no official distinctions by race, he wrote, "in practical application colored men are publically [sic] whipped and white men discharged on the payment of a small fine or giving bonds for future good conduct."[37] In Craven County, army and bureau officers accused the sheriff of failing to provide the freedmen with equal protection of the laws and of ignoring the bureau's request for assistance in cases in which crimes were allegedly committed by local whites against blacks. Such was the disregard of local officials for federal authority that on one occasion in 1866 the army adjutant at New Bern warned Sheriff Francis W. Harper that "in all cases where freedmen are concerned, you will recognize the authority of the agent of the Freedmen's Bureau and that any disregard on your part of his decisions or authority will subject you to arrest and trial."[38] Because of the president's control over national policy during the first two years after the war, the bureau increasingly limited its aid to blacks at James City and elsewhere to modest amounts of food and medical assistance.

With a limited capacity to help, bureau officials at the Trent River settlement strongly encouraged those freedmen able to make beneficial contracts to leave and seek employment on nearby plantations. These officers were especially anxious to find new homes for former slaves because it appeared that the land would soon be restored to its original white owners by the national government and the freedmen would be forced to move.[39]

A number of the black inhabitants heeded the advice of the bureau to leave the village, but most remained, preferring their existing circumstances to uncertain treatment on the plantations. In December, 1866, responding to orders from headquarters in Raleigh, Lieutenant Colonel Stephen Moore, the new subassistant commissioner for the Eastern District, canvassed the black community for those who might be departing. He found fifty families that intended to leave within the next month. In February, 1867, the freedmen in the camp numbered

---

[37] Colonel Eliphalet Whittlesey to Major General O. O. Howard, March 20, 1866, Letters Sent, Freedmen's Bureau Records, RG 105.

[38] Lieutenant J. H. Rollis to Francis W. Harper, February 17, 1866, Letters Sent, U.S. Army Continental Command, Department of North Carolina, RG 393, Letter Book 174/375, p. 22.

[39] Endorsements of Brevet Lieutenant Colonel Jacob F. Chur, November 21, December 4, 1866, Endorsements Sent, Freedmen's Bureau Records, RG 105.

1,760, a decrease of 242 since June, 1866. According to the camp superintendent, "about 100 have been hired out and will leave in a short time." They had departed by the first of May. During the same period 100 houses were demolished, leaving a total of 530 still occupied.[40]

For those freedmen willing to leave the settlement and become tenants on farms and plantations, wages ranged from $10.00 to $15.00 per month plus board for able-bodied men and $2.00 to $3.00 plus board for women. Ownership of land, however, remained the goal of most of the residents of James City. Lieutenant Colonel Moore remarked that "the majority of the freedmen work hard and earn an honest living. They have [an] intense desire to own land and often stand in their own light by working two or three acres of land for themselves in preference to hiring out to whites."

In June, 1867, the federal government restored to the Peter G. Evans family the area that included the Trent River settlement and the surrounding land farmed by the inhabitants.[41] By this time the conditions in the camp had deteriorated considerably. In the absence of the rents paid by the freedmen, those facilities which the sanitary inspector had found so neat and orderly in July, 1866, had fallen into disarray by June, 1867. One officer visiting the settlement at that time reported:

The hospital at Trent River I found in bad condition, the steward was engaged in having it whitewashed, and the employees were so few that the work progressed slowly, and the hospital wore a dirty appearance, the bread was sour, the coffee bad, the kitchen and furniture dirty and insufficient; there are not enough sheets for the patients now in the hospital and not nearly enough for a change, pillow slips and socks are required.

The officer recommended that a small amount of clothing be kept at the hospital for the benefit of the patients, "some of whom are as nearly naked as not to be decent, cleanliness will do as much or more than medicine for many of them, and it is impossible to keep them clean without a change of clothing." When the bureau restored the land to the white owners, the camp consisted of about 525 buildings and 180 acres of farmland.[42]

---

[40] Lieutenant Colonel Stephen Moore to Brevet Lieutenant Colonel Jacob F. Chur, December 29, 1866, February 2, 1867, Letters Sent, Freedmen's Bureau Records, RG 105; Monthly Report of Brevet Major General Nelson A. Miles on Abandoned Lands in his possession in the State of North Carolina during the Month Ending April 30, 1867, Land Division Records, Freedmen's Bureau Records, RG 105.

[41] Annual Report of the Sub-Assistant Commissioner of Sub-District 3, New Berne, September, 25, 1867, Reports of Operations (Annual), Freedmen's Bureau Records, RG 105.

[42] Lieutenant Robert Avery to Assistant Commissioner for North Carolina, June 19, 1867, Registered Letters Received, Freedmen's Bureau Records, RG 105.

In October, 1867, General Nelson A. Miles, assistant commissioner for North Carolina, wrote to General Howard that "since the last annual report all the colonies have been broken up and the properties upon which they are settled restored to the owners. This has been accomplished by gradual, systematic measures resulting in no disadvantage or suffering to the former occupants." Miles was not entirely correct, for although all the other freedmen's camps in North Carolina, including Roanoke Island, had been abolished by this date, James City remained intact.[43]

Most of the inhabitants of the James City camp elected to remain where they were. They agreed to pay rent to the white owners for their lots in the camp and to work as farm laborers or to farm as sharecroppers for the Evanses and other area planters. Those who chose sharecropping divided the crop evenly with their white partners in cases in which they supplied half the seed and animal feed. When planters provided everything but the labor, the freedmen received one third of the crop. Census data for Craven County reveal that by 1870 most of the employed inhabitants among the approximately 1,500 blacks who then populated James City were farm laborers. The next largest group consisted of farmers who either sharecropped or tilled rented land. Others were fishermen, laborers, boatmen, coopers, blacksmiths, sawmill workers, shingle makers, domestic servants, nurses, and housewives. Under their rental agreement with the white owners of the settlement, they paid between 25 cents and $1.00 per month for their lots in the village—a total of $2,400 a year for the entire population.

Bureau officers attempted to persuade the Evans family to sell the James City lots and small plots of land to those freedmen who could raise sufficient money. The family refused. In 1865 former governor John M. Morehead, grandfather of the Evans heirs, went so far as to ask bureau officials to assist his family by collecting rents from the settlement; the bureau declined to do so.[44]

The change to the sharecrop system brought a significant decline in the standard of living for residents of James City. As previously mentioned, while under the guidance of the bureau the freedmen had farmed

---

[43] Brevet Major General Nelson A. Miles to Major General O. O. Howard, October 9, 1867, Letters Sent, Freedmen's Bureau Records, RG 105.

[44] Report from the Eastern District, October 30, 1866, Reports of Operations (Annual), Freedmen's Bureau Records, RG 105; Colonel Eliphalet Whittlesey to Brigadier General J. A. Campbell, May 7, 1866, Lieutenant Colonel Stephen Moore to Brevet Lieutenant Colonel Jacob F. Chur, February 24, 1868, and Farmers' Association to Moore, February 19, 1868, all in Registered Letters Received, Freedmen's Bureau Records, RG 105; Ninth Census of the United States, 1870: Craven County, North Carolina, Population Schedule, 371-425, microfilm of National Archives manuscript copy, State Archives.

their own land and enjoyed the income from their entire crop. This made them virtually self-sufficient. But one half or one third of a crop was often not enough to elevate them to the subsistence level that they had maintained at the beginning of Reconstruction. Furthermore, in a number of cases the tenants received nothing after a year's labor because the white planters were in debt and creditors took the entire crop. Moreover, because blacks had little recourse in local courts, some white planters found it easy to cheat the freedmen of their share of the crop. Some planters cited rumors of impending black insurrection as evidence that freedmen should not be trusted or treated fairly.[45]

The blacks of James City saw their fortunes steadily deteriorate, and they were in need of assistance as never before. To improve their situation, Baptist minister Hurley Grimes in January, 1868, led the community to form the Farmers Association of James City and drew up a set of resolutions that were sent to General Howard. The resolutions read in part:

... the Trent River Settlement ... has come down to poverty for the want of provision. We then as a band of brethren fearing God have assembled ourselves together to adopt these resolutions by calling upon the United States to aid us in the mighty struggle. No other help do we know. The conservatives are no friends to us they will neither employ nor help us in no shape and we believe that God will bless the United States for her aid and support to the poor and will enable her to conquer all governments upon the surface of the earth and by showing love and charity to the poor. . . .

... we pledge ourselves to the performance of every honorable duty characteristic of good citizenship that all reports to the effect that we are trying to evoke a war of races are base falsehood and have only been circulated for the purpose of retarding reconstruction and the peaceful settlement of national troubles. . . .

Many of us cultivated farms last year with the conservative people and when the crop was ended they was so much indebted to others they did not pay us for our labor, and many of their crops has been taken by the sheriff and sold from them before we got any pay so that leaves us in a bad condition. We believe that the U.S. Government will look on our condition with all tenderness so much as can be expected. We cannot live very well unless we have some asset from a better friend than they or ourselves. . . .

We thought that we should never be oblige[d] to call upon the U.S. Gov. but poverty has driven us to this. It has been said that we would not work but these resolution[s] will show to country [sic].

---

[45] Colonel Eliphalet Whittlesey to Major General O. O. Howard, March 20, 1865, Letters Sent, Freedmen's Bureau Records, RG 105; Monthly Report for the State of North Carolina for the Month Ending December 28, 1865, Statistical Reports of Operations, Freedmen's Bureau Records, RG 105; Sheriff James E. Fleming to Major J. J. Van Horne, January 6, 1866, Letters Received, U.S. Army Continental Command, Department of North Carolina, RG 393, Letter Book 174/375, pp. 127-128.

The Reverend Hurley Grimes, pastor of the Mount Shiloh First Baptist Church, was an important religious and civic leader in the James City community. This photograph of Grimes was found in the attic of the Mount Shiloh Church in 1980.

The members of the association were quick to point out that they were well aware of the political situation in the South and the nation and that their support and interest lay with Congress. They firmly asserted that in return for their support they expected the Republican party to act in behalf of their interests. They declared that "the government should not expect our support in any form until she guarantees to us every right and privilege secured to other citizens and that upon such provision we are willing to die in her defence" and resolved to "tender our sincere thanks to the Congress of the U.S. for its persistent efforts to establish uniform Justice to all men." The association ended the resolutions by proclaiming that "we ask nothing at the hands of the nation but equal Justice in common with other men and nothing else will ever satisfy or console our people."[46]

As a consequence of the James City petition the bureau ordered an investigation of the plight of the inhabitants. When Subassistant Commissioner Stephen Moore received orders from Raleigh instructing him to investigate conditions at the camp, he became incensed that the Farmers Association had appealed directly to his superiors. In a defensive position, Moore wrote bureau headquarters at Raleigh that the people of the Trent River settlement were no more destitute than other blacks in his district and were grumbling unjustifiably; nevertheless, he did request rations for those needing them. In an effort to soothe his injured feelings, the Farmers Association sent Moore a letter of apology

---

[46] "Resolutions of Farmers' Association at James City," enclosed in Colonel Eliphalet Whittlesey to Brevet Major General Nelson A. Miles, February 5, 1868, Registered Letters Received, Freedmen's Bureau Records, RG 105, hereinafter cited as "Resolutions of Farmers' Association."

for going over his head but reiterated that what they had said was true.[47]

Some of the freedmen refused to acknowledge that the federal government had relinquished to the original owners title to the land on which many of them had resided since 1863. They insisted that during the war the government had given them the tracts on which they lived and worked, and they felt that they would eventually obtain clear legal title to these properties. They referred to the camp as the "promised land"—promised to them, they claimed, by the United States in return for their services as Union soldiers and as a reparation for their years in slavery. Some refused to pay rent to the Evanses and continued to insist that the land was theirs. They were reinforced in their opinion by news that a number of national leaders, such as Congressman Thaddeus Stevens of Pennsylvania, had declared that the freedmen should have the lands of former "rebels."

Those blacks who refused to recognize the Johnson administration's relinquishment of the property maintained that the same government that had granted them freedom should have no trouble in giving them small plots of land. After all, they reasoned, the United States had won the war and could do whatever it wanted with the spoils. In addition, the initial experience of blacks during Reconstruction had demonstrated that they could survive on their own if they possessed land from which they could reap the benefits of the harvest. In light of this, they asked, why should they have to give up their land and homes—the first they could really call their own?[48]

At the end of 1868 the Freedmen's Bureau terminated all aid to the inhabitants of James City and within a few months departed the state.[49] During the early stages of Reconstruction the bureau had rendered to former slaves at the camp valuable services in the form of rations,

---

[47] Lieutenant Colonel Stephen Moore to Brevet Lieutenant Colonel Jacob F. Chur, February 24, 1868, and Farmers' Association to Moore, February 19, 1868, Registered Letters Received, Freedmen's Bureau Records, RG 105.

[48] "Resolutions of Farmers' Association"; Lieutenant Colonel Stephen Moore to Brevet Lieutenant Colonel Jacob F. Chur, February 24, 1868, Registered Letters Received, Freedmen's Bureau Records, RG 105; Craven County Deeds, Office of the Register of Deeds, Craven County Courthouse, New Bern, Book 85, p. 433, hereinafter cited as Craven County Deeds; author's interview with Isaac Long, James City, March 24, 1980 (notes on interview in possession of author), hereinafter cited as Long interview, March 24, 1980. Mr. Long, who lived in James City during the late nineteenth century, recalls overhearing his parents and others who resided there during Reconstruction conversing about the freedmen's having to relinquish the property.

[49] Report of the Assistant Commissioner for the Quarter ending November, 1868, in Reports of Rations Issued and Related Records, Freedmen's Bureau Records, RG 105; Zuber, North Carolina during Reconstruction, 6.

medical attention, and education. But its greatest contribution was in providing land upon which the freedmen were able to gain an economic foothold amid the turmoil of the postwar period. The gift was, however, temporary, and the success of the freedmen was short-lived. After two years of Reconstruction, national policy dictated the return of the James City land to its prewar owners. As a result, the former slaves lost the economic independence that land ownership had given them. They then assumed the status of laborer or sharecropper, which would be their lot for years to come. Yet they were no longer slaves, and for the time being they had the privilege of the ballot and modest civil rights. With knowledge of this, the citizens of James City faced the future.

IV. JAMES CITY, 1870-1900

When the Freedmen's Bureau left North Carolina, the people of James City were forced to rely totally upon their own resources. But their brief ownership of land and economic self-sufficiency had taught them valuable lessons of independence. Armed with this experience, they clung to their sense of community with tenacious determination to survive.

James City blacks remained politically active and continued to support the party that had brought them out of slavery. They were committed during the 1870s to the presidency of Ulysses S. Grant, whom they viewed as a liberator second only to Abraham Lincoln. They exhibited their devotion in 1872 when liberal Republicans nominated Horace Greeley to run against Grant, the incumbent, for president. During the campaign an election official for the liberal, or independent, Republicans rowed across the Trent River to James City for the purpose of persuading blacks to vote for Greeley. A newspaper correspondent described what took place when the election official arrived at the black settlement:

After announcing to the assembled multitude that he was an independent Republican, he awaited developments. There were no developments. The residents of James City had never heard of an independent Republican. They had heard of Republicans and Democrats, but beyond these they had no knowledge of political partisans. Before they proceeded to extremities they desired to obtain further information from the stranger. The latter explained that as an independent Republican he advocated the election as President of Horace Greeley and the defeat of General Grant. He was accounted a fine[?] speaker and would probably have said more had he considered the time and place propitious. His audience, having grasped the fact that the stranger was opposed to General Grant moved upon the ex-judge with so much celerity and earnestness that he was barely able to get a start of five yards. As the friends of General Grant got between him and his boat the stranger made a straight break for the Trent River. The river at the point chosen by the ex-judge is nearly a mile wide. He waded out to his chin and then informed the friends of Greeley on the opposite bank if they had any patriotism in their souls they would rescue him from his bloodthirsty pursuers. They rescued him and since that time the people of James City have been utterly neglected by independent Republican and Democratic orators.[1]

James City blacks further displayed their devotion to the Republican party when President James A. Garfield died at the hands of an assassin in 1881. When the news of his murder reached James City, the inhabi-

---

[1] *New York Times*, April 9, 1888.

tants held a memorial service at the Jones A.M.E. Zion Chapel. The "Reverend Holt," a James City minister, opened the ceremonies "with an appropriate hymn." The Reverend Amos York from New Bern preached a sermon from 2 Samuel—"there is a prince and a great man fallen." The community recalled Garfield as a Union general, an anti-slavery man, and a friend of blacks in the South.[2]

Following the elections of 1876, Reconstruction in North Carolina and throughout the South ended and "home rule" was restored. Although the Democratic party regained control of the state government, Republicans in Craven County, like their counterparts in other areas having a majority of black voters, still managed to elect their party's candidates, including blacks, to local offices. The people of James City continued to vote in their own interest and from 1868 to 1900 helped to elect to the state legislature fourteen blacks from Craven County. As residents of the Second Congressional District, known as the "Black Second," they also helped to elect four Negroes who served in Congress from that district: James E. O'Hara, Henry P. Cheatham, John A. Hyman, and George H. White. Black candidates were generally successful in winning election to county offices, although in 1877 the state legislature attempted to limit the number of blacks in local government by enacting the so-called County Government System. Under this scheme the legislature, dominated by Democrats, was able to control the various county governments through its power to appoint key county officials.[3]

According to historian Frenise A. Logan, "in most, if not all, of the elections in North Carolina between 1876 and 1894, Negroes who voted with Democrats were subjected to ostracism by their own race."[4] This was certainly true in James City, for the first black resident to vote Democratic was burned in effigy and run out of the community. "We made a tar man and burned it up," one member of the community recalled. "We felt he was set up by the white man." When a number of black former Republicans became affiliated with the third-party Populists during the 1890s, the people of James City continued to support Republican candidates such as Daniel L. Russell, who was elected governor in 1896.[5]

[2] *Commercial News* (New Bern), September 28, 1881, hereinafter cited as *Commercial News*.

[3] Frenise A. Logan, *The Negro in North Carolina, 1876-1894* (Chapel Hill: University of North Carolina Press, 1964), 9-10, 30-32, hereinafter cited as Logan, *The Negro in North Carolina*; Lefler and Newsome, *North Carolina*, 551; Eric Anderson, *Race and Politics in North Carolina, 1872-1901: The Black Second* (Baton Rouge: Louisiana State University Press, 1981), 56-57; Craven County Election Records and Returns.

[4] Logan, *The Negro in North Carolina*, 22-23.

[5] Long interview, March 24, 1980; Craven County Election Records and Returns.

Several residents of James City were elected to local offices. Washington Spivey, a farmer and merchant, was elected constable of Craven County Township No. Seven. He also became postmaster in 1888 when Republican representatives in the national government attempted to enhance their political standing among blacks by awarding certain federal positions, especially that of postmaster, to influential blacks in the South. Spivey, as did other blacks from James City, served as a justice of the peace during the 1890s when local self-government had been restored to the counties by a state legislature temporarily controlled by a coalition, or "fusion," of Republicans and Populists.[6] Spivey's store became a meeting place for local residents, who viewed the merchant as the community's leader. Spivey took eggs and other farm products in trade for supplies. He purchased cotton from James City farmers and extended them credit until they could bring in a crop.[7]

In 1880 approximately 1,100 blacks lived in James City. Females in the community outnumbered males by 622 to 478. The Craven County census indicates that all able-bodied adults were employed in some capacity. Farm laborers, numbering 281, constituted the largest group of employed inhabitants. "House keepers," numbering 133, made up the second-largest group, and other important occupations were shingler (30), laborer (29), and fisherman (27). Two hundred eighty-three women were employed at occupations other than "keeping house." The majority of these were farm laborers. Other occupations for women included cook, domestic servant, schoolteacher, seamstress, store clerk, "clerk for hucksters," peddler, and nurse. (For a complete list of occupations followed by the people of James City in 1880, see Appendix, Table 6.) The 1880 census shows that both father and mother (having the same last name) were present in almost all households in which there were children. Adult males were listed as heads of a large majority of the 305 households. The largest number of children in any one household in James City in 1880 was eight, but few households then had more than five.[8]

---

[6] Logan, *The Negro in North Carolina*, 5, 44, 47; Records of the United States Post Office Department, 1789-1929, Records of Appointments of Postmasters for North Carolina, Appointments for Craven County, 1877-1889, Record Group 28, p. 102, microfilm of National Archives manuscript copy, State Archives; Craven County Board of Commissioners, Minutes, Volume 5 (1889-1896), pp. 284-285, Craven County Courthouse, New Bern, hereinafter cited as Craven County Commissioners' Minutes, with appropriate volume and page numbers.

[7] Long interview, March 24, 1980.

[8] Tenth Census of the United States, 1880: Craven County, North Carolina, Population Schedule, 211-232, microfilm of National Archives manuscript copy, State Archives, hereinafter cited as Tenth Census, 1880, Craven County, Population Schedule, with appropriate page numbers.

The citizens of the settlement had placed a strong emphasis on education, but with the restoration of Democratic home rule they feared that
state expenditures for the instruction of their children would be brought
to an end. To demonstrate their concern, they attended, on October 1,
1877, a black convention at the courthouse in New Bern. This meeting
was called to "take into consideration their educational status and to appoint delegates to a like convention, to assemble in Raleigh October
18th" for the purpose of inducing the state government to support black
education. The New Bern press applauded these efforts of local blacks,
but with reservations. "This is a move in the right direction," declared
one editor,

... and we are glad to see that our colored friends throughout the State are wak-
ing up to the advantages of education, and are beginning to appreciate the fact
that "knowledge is power." If they would only for the present time give less
thought to politics; would only cut loose from their bad advisers and fit themselves by proper training for independent thought and the cares and responsibilities of citizenship it would be better for all concerned.

The editor also claimed that the Democrats, not the "radical"
Republicans, had the interest of blacks at heart and were responsible for
whatever educational advantages they possessed.[9] Despite the
enthusiastic participation by James City blacks, such efforts as the New
Bern convention accomplished little in the way of improving educational opportunities in the village.

During the 1880s three black teachers operated a public school in
James City. The students attended classes for four months at a cost to
the state of $300. The attendance ranged between 130 and 170. In 1888
George Willis, the principal, received $35.00 per month in salary. His
first assistant, Georgie Davis, had a salary of $25.00, and the primary
teacher, Nancy Walker, received $20.00. One traveler recorded a visit to
the school:

The school is a curiosity and cost probably $200. It is two stories in height,
built of boards, and has a brick chimney which begins at the second story. The
chimney is laid on the floor and is connected with the ground floor by a stove
pipe. It naturally originates a fire on the second floor when the weather is cool
enough for a blaze in the iron stove on the ground floor, but so far these con-
flagrations have always been quickly extinguished by the scholars, who have
been organized as a fire brigade.

The traveler noted that none of the students had a complete set of books

---

[9] *Newbernian* (New Bern), September 8, 22, October 6, 1877, hereinafter cited as *Newbernian.*

Isaac Long, who was born in James City in 1886, recalls attending school there during the 1890s. In the course of several extensive interviews with the author in 1980, Mr. Long displayed a remarkable ability to describe events connected with his youth. Photograph (1980) by Walton Haywood; from the files of the Division of Archives and History.

and that they were weak in geography because the school had no maps. But "in spite of the disadvantages under which they labor some of them seemed to possess wonderful memories and they reeled off lengthy answers to some questions . . . with amazing glibness." Arithmetic was a strong point and "on the whole they did as well as white children under the same conditions would have done, perhaps better." [10] Isaac Long, who attended the school during the 1890s when he was taught by Nancy Walker, remembers that he learned from "the old blue back speller." [11] The 1900 census reveals that in Township No. Seven, which included James City, only three blacks were educated beyond the third grade. Over half of the approximately 2,000 blacks who resided in the township were listed as being able to read and write. [12]

Five churches remained influential in the black community after Reconstruction, and the congregations looked to their ministers for leadership. Because the churches were the focal points for the settlement, they received the largest share of its devotion, both financial and spiritual. A correspondent reported that they were "well attended" and that all the "church buildings are quite respectable-looking and quite comfortable." [13] Whites in the New Bern area generally approved of the churches' influence on blacks. On one occasion B. A. Ball, a white silver-

---

[10] New York Times, April 9, 1888.
[11] Long interview, March 24, 1980.
[12] Twelfth Census of the United States, 1900: Craven County, North Carolina, Population Schedule, 107-127, microfilm of National Archives manuscript copy, State Archives, hereinafter cited as Twelfth Census, 1900, Craven County, Population Schedule, with appropriate page numbers.
[13] New York Times, April 9, 1888.

smith and jeweler, donated a clock to the Jones A.M.E. Zion Chapel in James City. "We cannot express our gratitude and warm thanks toward the gentleman [Ball] enough," wrote elder S. B. Hunter to the *Newbernian* in 1878.[14] Whites did not, however, approve of the activities of black ministers such as Hurley Grimes, who organized the Farmers Association of James City and may have been a leader in an 1881 labor strike. According to local tradition, the Reverend Grimes fell dead while delivering a sermon in the Mount Shiloh First Baptist Church in 1888. His passing was marked by much grief in the black settlement.[15]

A strong sense of community cooperation became manifest in James City on September 18, 1881, when, as a protest against the low wages paid by white landowners to black laborers and the high prices charged by local merchants, the farm laborers in the village began a strike for higher wages. Apparently having met previously and agreed to act jointly, the laborers distributed in New Bern handbills declaring that in the future they would not pick cotton for less than 1 cent per pound or work for less than 50 cents a day. The going rate was then half a cent a pound. The workers (including the women, who were active participants in the strike) threatened to prevent other blacks in the New Bern vicinity from breaking the strike by working for less than the proposed wage. In order to enforce the strike, many of the James City cotton pickers went to New Bern on the day after the boycott was declared.[16] At that time two planters, A. B. Dawson of China Grove plantation and Bruce Ipock of Core Creek, were in the town with wagons to transport black laborers to their cotton fields for work. But the James City workers prevented the loaded wagons from leaving. According to an account of the incident published in the *Commercial News*, "The teams were stopped in the street by an excited mob, and men and women dragged from the wagons and their baggage scattered in the streets. Threats of violence to persons and property were freely indulged." Apparently no one was seriously injured in spite of any such threats to the contrary.

The action by the James City laborers outraged whites in and around New Bern. The editor of the *Commercial News* declared that "we are very sorry to hear that a minister of the gospel [Israel B. Abbott?] was prominent in this affair, and that others from whom better things were to have been expected were engaged in aiding and encouraging intimidation and open violation of the law."

---

[14] *Newbernian*, February 16, 1878.
[15] *Commercial News*, September 20, 1881; author's interview with James C. Delemar, James City, April 16, 1980 (notes on interview in possession of author), hereinafter cited as Delemar interview, April 16, 1980.
[16] *Commercial News*, September 18, 1881.

Some of the colored people [the editor wrote] seem determined to drive from them the countenance and encouragement of all good people, both white and black, and to make it impossible for any body to do anything for them to benefit their condition. They will not be guided by their own common sense, or the advice of the better men of their own race, and if a white man attempts to befriend them, they leave him no ground to stand upon.

If any do not choose to work for the wages offered they have perfect right to do so, but when they attempt to prevent others, they are guilty of an outrage which no decent man of any race can tolerate, and as violators of the law they will be punished as they deserve.

Cotton prices were declining, claimed the editor, "and the refusal of the Labor of this section to assist in marketing our crop in time to realize best prices, is cutting its own throat."[17]

The James City strikers were led by Israel B. Abbott, a black preacher of New Bern, who published a newspaper called the *Lodge* "in the interest of colored people." The newspaper urged black workers in all occupations to organize labor unions for the regulation of wages.[18] Along with black ministers John S. Tucker and E. E. Tucker, Abbott addressed the striking laborers at a meeting at Red Church on West Street in New Bern on the afternoon of September 18, 1881. The ministers condemned the violence that had occurred earlier that day and declared that they did not want to create trouble between employers and labor but desired only fair wages for blacks. A lack of cooperation from other blacks and economic necessity soon forced the strikers to return to the fields, where the white planters were "paying fifty cents per hundred [pounds of cotton picked], and are getting nearly as much labor as they want." On October 4 the *Commercial News* noted: "Several wagon loads of cotton pickers left for the country yesterday, from which we infer the temporary disturbance of that labor [strike] has passed off, and the farmers will now get their staple to market without further trouble."[19]

Low wages, combined with legal and political restraints enacted into law by the newly established Democratic regime, led some residents of James City to consider leaving North Carolina. Beginning in 1879 there was a general exodus of blacks from the state to the Midwest, especially to Kansas and Indiana. Such migrations occurred throughout the South, and the black emigrants were often called "exodusters." A great shortage of labor then existed in the midwestern states, which in general accorded to blacks more economic, political, and legal freedom than did states in the "redeemed" Democratic South. Some blacks in North

---

[17] *Commercial News*, September 20, 1881.
[18] *Commercial News*, September 18, 1881.
[19] *Commercial News*, September 21, 29, October 4, 1881.

Beginning about 1879, large numbers of blacks in North Carolina and other southern states began migrating to the Midwest in search of better economic and social conditions. This engraving shows a group of North Carolina blacks gathered at a railroad station to await the arrival of a train to take them to the Midwest. From *Frank Leslie's Illustrated Newspaper*, February 15, 1890.

Carolina at this time planned to emigrate to Liberia in Africa, but no evidence exists that those living in James City considered such a move.[20]

Whites in the New Bern area opposed any exodus that might deprive them of a labor force and attempted to frighten blacks into staying. The white press warned the blacks that they would fall victim to starvation, disease, bandits, and unsympathetic employers if they left the state. The *Newbernian* in 1879 even warned the residents of James City that if they migrated to the Midwest they would be murdered by "body-snatchers" who provided the region's medical schools with black cadavers for dissection.[21]

In 1881 the inhabitants of James City held meetings "to hear speeches delivered upon the subject of emigration" and to decide if they should leave the New Bern area en masse for some other part of the country. They apparently desired to stay together as a colony if they did move. Some wanted to leave in the hope of gaining ownership of land. Many of them cited the rents they had to pay for homesites as an additional reason for leaving. But the meetings led to no mass emigration. Although a few of James City's blacks may have departed to seek better opportunities, most of them rejected the lure of Kansas or other places; they preferred the safety and stability of an imperfect yet cohesive black community to the uncertainty of a journey into the unknown.[22]

[20] Logan, *The Negro in North Carolina*, 117-135; Nell Irvin Painter, *Exodusters: Black Migration to Kansas after Reconstruction* (New York: Alfred A. Knopf, 1976), 138.
[21] *Newbernian*, December 27, 1879.
[22] *Commercial News*, October 27, 1881.

Living conditions in James City were comparable to those under which most blacks in the area lived. "The average colored man of James City," reported a correspondent in 1888, "is no better or no worse off than the colored man—speaking in a general sense—of any other part of the eastern coast." The inhabitants of the settlement improved the shanties built during the war and Reconstruction or replaced them with more substantial structures. Most households had garden plots nearby, and some residents had large truck gardens "in the rear of the town" from which they sold produce such as peas, beans, cabbage, corn, and other vegetables. Some also raised small crops of cotton or tobacco for additional income. Fish from the Neuse and Trent rivers were a part of their diet and were sold to supplement their wages. Many families owned some type of boat for fishing and for transportation to New Bern.

During the late nineteenth century many residents of James City supplemented their incomes by selling fish caught in the Trent or Neuse rivers. Shown above is a fish market in New Bern. Photograph (ca. 1900) from Emma H. Powell, *New Bern* (N.p.: n.p., c. 1905), p. 31.

The Clermont Bridge (named for nearby Clermont plantation), which connected New Bern with James City, was frequently in disrepair, and the only other way to cross the Trent River was by boat or ferry, which often involved a fee. A portion of the railroad bridge that had once been used by wagons and pedestrians had fallen into disrepair and by the 1880s was no longer passable.[23]

[23] *New York Times*, April 9, 1888; Delemar interview, April 16, 1980; Craven County Commissioners' Minutes, Volume 1 (1868-1874), pp. 170, 524, Volume 3 (1878-1884), p. 18, Volume 6 (1896-1902), pp. 149-150.

The people of James City held regular social events during the late nineteenth century. Beginning soon after the Civil War, they celebrated Emancipation Day on January 1 of every year. They also celebrated May 30 as a memorial day for the blacks of the community who had served in the African Brigade during the war. Blacks from outlying areas and other counties usually came to the settlement to commemorate these events.[24]

The churches of the community were the center of social life. They frequently held revivals and prayer meetings that were accompanied by picnics, games, and socializing. Blacks from other areas attended these affairs in large numbers. In describing one such event in 1881, a New Bern newspaper reported that "from Beaufort and Morehead City a train of four or five cars arrived in the morning bringing some two hundred and fifty or three hundred." From the eastern counties over a thousand blacks were preparing to come to the celebration, "necessitating the dispatching of an extra train as far up as Kinston, and both from that direction came in at noon, crowded." According to the newspaper, "the excursionists passed the afternoon in a very pleasant and becoming manner."[25]

Recreational pastimes also included fishing, baseball, dances, parades, picnics, and band concerts. Music was provided by a band under the leadership of Alexander Delemar, a former slave. Delemar's band developed an excellent reputation throughout eastern North

Alexander Delemar, a former slave and resident of James City, achieved renown in the black communities of eastern North Carolina as the organizer and leader of a talented band. Delemar's band became a fixture at local social events and even provided music for funerals. Photograph courtesy James C. Delemar, James City.

---

[24] Long interview, March 24, 1980; Delemar interview, March 24, 1980.
[25] *Commercial News*, October 18, 1881.

Carolina for its talent and even played for funerals—which were held, according to one resident, "in a New Orleans fashion." The graveyard where the deceased of James City were buried was on the outskirts of the village; it had originated as a slave cemetery on the Clermont plantation. At the conclusion of a funeral, mourners and Delemar's band followed the casket on the route to the graveyard. The band played spirituals, and one of the favorites was "Safe in the Arms of Jesus." [26]

An appointed constable for Township No. Seven was responsible for law and order in the community. He was usually from James City.[27] An unofficial committee of the village's twelve leading citizens (called the Committee of Twelve), elected by the residents, made most legal and governmental decisions involving the community. This local government by committee may have been an outgrowth of a policy initiated by Horace James to allow a committee of freedmen a voice in making decisions on matters affecting the Trent River camp.

In 1880 the heirs of Colonel Peter G. Evans sold 618 acres of land—which included the James City property—to Mary S. Bryan of New Bern.[28] Mrs. Bryan was the wife of James A. Bryan, member of a large and prominent landowning family. Bryan had served as a captain in the Confederate army but immediately after the Civil War had proclaimed his loyalty to the Union. Because he had owned more than $20,000 worth of property before the war, he was obliged to apply for a special pardon from President Johnson. He submitted his petition on June 19, 1865, professing that "my sympathies were never with the so-called Confederate Government . . . & I can . . . say without fear of contradiction that my relations with the Davis Government were a matter of necessity & not of choice." [29]

In the postwar years Bryan added thousands of acres to his already large landholdings in Craven and surrounding counties. He also became president of the state-controlled Atlantic & North Carolina Railroad, a portion of which ran through James City, and served as president of the National Bank of New Bern from 1880 until his death in 1923. He was elected as a Democrat to the 1899 state Senate and earlier "was in-

[26] Author's interviews with Isaac Long, James C. Delemar, and Mary Etta Hill Delmar (Mrs. Delmar spells her surname without the second e), March 14, 24, 1980.
[27] See, for example, Craven County Commissioners' Minutes, Volume 1, p. 49, and Volume 3, p. 470.
[28] E. W. Carpenter, clerk of the Superior Court of Craven County, to Mary S. Bryan, October 1, 1880, Craven County Deeds, Book 82, pp. 431-432, microfilm copy, State Archives, hereinafter cited as Craven County Deeds.
[29] Petition of James A. Bryan, June 19, 1865, Petitions for Pardons, 1865-1868, Box 1, Military Collection, Civil War Collection, 1861-1865, State Archives.

strumental in helping relieve Craven County from Reconstruction policies."[30]

Upon acquiring the James City property, Bryan began systematically to collect rents from the inhabitants. Evidently he was more conscientious in this effort than had been the Evanses. The people of James City later claimed that they had paid no rent to the Evans heirs since September, 1867. The neglect of the previous landlords in collecting rents led many James City blacks to chafe under Bryan's more persistent efforts. Having earlier abandoned the idea of an exodus, the blacks offered Bryan $2,000 for 600 acres, including James City. He declined their offer.[31]

Weary of trying to collect the rents and harboring speculative plans for the sale of the land, Bryan soon attempted to evict the blacks from James City. When they refused to go, he brought suit against them in Craven County Superior Court in October, 1881. The people of James City, led by Washington Spivey, contested Bryan's legal right to force them off the land. They hired lawyers and vigorously developed their defense. They argued that they were entitled to remain at James City by virtue of the legal right of adverse possession—having lived there unmolested since 1867 when, they claimed, the Freedmen's Bureau gave them the land.[32] (It should be recalled that the Freedmen's Bureau returned the site to the Evans heirs in June, 1867, and informed the people in the Trent River camp that it was taking that action.)

In an effort to strengthen their case against Bryan, the inhabitants of the black settlement in 1882 produced a deed purportedly made in 1867 and proceeded to have it recorded at the Craven County Courthouse. The deed indicated that the "committee of twelve" collectively had sold the land in September, 1867, to James Salter, a James City man. Salter then sold or deeded portions of the property to individual residents in order that they would have title to their plots. The committee appointed to transfer the property to Salter declared in the document

That the United States gave us [the land and] told us not to pay rent to anyone; and whereas the said tract of land was given to 12 of us as a committee [by] the authority of the others, we do bargain and sell all the said land, except lots [that] have been bought by same [James Salter], from parties that have moved and [sold] their lots and gave deeds for the same.

---

[30] William S. Powell (ed.), *Dictionary of North Carolina Biography* (Chapel Hill: University of North Carolina Press [projected multivolume series, 1979—]), I, 225, hereinafter cited as Powell, *DNCB*.

[31] *Commercial News*, October 27, 1881.

[32] *James A. Bryan and Mary S. Bryan v. Washington Spivey et al.*, 109 N.C. 57 (1891), hereinafter cited as *Bryan and Bryan v. Spivey* (1891).

The fifteen-year lapse of time notwithstanding, Probate Judge Edward W. Carpenter, formerly of New York, ordered the deed recorded.[33] Carpenter, a Republican, enjoyed strong political support from the voters of James City.[34]

Despite Bryan's efforts to have the case tried immediately, the people of James City managed to delay court action until 1889 by periodically pleading the absence of important witnesses or attorneys. During the time the trial was pending they prepared their case and continued to live and work as they had before the suit, apparently paying no rent.[35] At one time one of their attorneys was, ironically, Furnifold M. Simmons, a man who would eventually work for disfranchisement of blacks in North Carolina and the rule of white supremacy. Simmons later became a United States senator and head of the Democratic party in North Carolina.

The case of *James A. Bryan* v. *Washington Spivey et al.* finally came to trial in the fall, 1889, term of Craven County Superior Court. Upon a motion by the defendants, the court ruled that each landholder in James City was entitled to a separate trial. The court based its action on the ground that a number of the defendants held legal title to their lots on the basis of the Salter deed recorded in 1882.[36]

This ruling, if it withstood the appeal process, meant that in order for Bryan to evict the residents of James City and resume full control of the property in question, he would have to confront each landholder in a separate trial—a process that would require an inordinant amount of time and effort. Whether or not the citizens of James City had recorded the deed to James Salter in 1882 partly in the hope of gaining separate trials is not certain. But there is little doubt that once the document was recorded, they used it in an attempt to hinder Bryan by forcing him to evict them one at a time. As might be expected, Bryan appealed the ruling for separate trials to the state supreme court, and in 1890 this body overturned the decision of the lower court, denying the right of the black contestants to separate trials.[37]

---

[33] Southey B. Hunter and others to James Salter and others, September 25, 1867 [recorded June 20, 1882], Craven County Deeds, Book 85, pp. 433-434.

[34] Craven County Election Records. See specifically Volume C.R. 028.912.1.

[35] *James A. Bryan and Mary S. Bryan* v. *Washington Spivey, Caroline Alexander, et al.*, Craven County Civil Actions Concerning Land, 1891-1894, Box C.R. 028.325.76, State Archives.

[36] Craven County Superior Court, Minutes, Fall Term, 1889, Volume D, p. 558. See also *James A. Bryan and Wife* v. *Washington Spivey et al.*, Case No. 16,232, Supreme Court Original Cases, 1800-1909, Box 736, State Archives, hereinafter cited as *Bryan and Wife* v. *Spivey*, Supreme Court Original Cases.

[37] *James A. Bryan and Wife* v. *Washington Spivey et al.*, 106 N.C. 95 (1890).

When the case of *Bryan* v. *Spivey et al.* was tried in Craven County Superior Court in February, 1891, the court decided in favor of Bryan, and the residents of James City appealed the case to the state supreme court. In September the supreme court upheld the lower court decision and awarded the land to Bryan, arguing that because the Evans and Bryan families held legal title the defendants could not claim adverse possession of the settlement.[38]

Following this decision the people of James City tried once again to keep their homesites. In 1892 they filed a "petition for betterments" with the Craven County Superior Court. Under this petition they sought to recover the cost of the improvements they had made to the land. They listed these improvements as the laying out of streets and lots; the building of churches, schools, and 500 dwellings; the improvement of the soil by fertilizing; and the planting of "valuable fruit and shade trees." In compensation for the cost of these improvements the residents asked for $50,000 from Bryan, "over and above the use and occupation of said lands," and that a lien be placed on the James City tracts in order to permit them to recover that sum. If the court allowed their petition, they could claim the land—providing Bryan refused to pay them $50,000 for the improvements they had made. The court ruled against the petition, and again the residents appealed to the state supreme court. In September, 1892, the court denied the "petition for betterments," declaring that because the defendants had not resided on the land "under color of title," they had no claim to compensation for improvements. The court reaffirmed its decision that Bryan was owner of the James City property and that the black residents had no legal grounds for ownership.[39]

Having been awarded title to the land, Bryan set out to evict the tenants. He already had in mind several schemes for using the 618 acres of Evans land, which included the approximately 180 acres utilized by the inhabitants of James City. One native of the town told a newcomer that "everything there not always belonging to God is now owned by Jim Bryan."[40]

The so-called "squatters" of the black community, however, refused to comply with Bryan's demands that they remove themselves. Some continued to insist that the land was theirs, given to them by the Freedmen's Bureau. Most acknowledged the court's decision to award the property to Bryan but felt that he should be required to sell them the

---

[38] *Bryan and Bryan* v. *Spivey* (1891).

[39] *James A. Bryan and Wife* v. *Caroline Alexander*, 111 N.C. 142 (1892); *Bryan and Wife* v. *Spivey*, Supreme Court Original Cases.

[40] Powell, *DNCB*, I, 255.

tracts on which they lived because of the length of time they had resided there. Others refused to leave unless they were compensated for the improvements they had made to the property, especially the construction of buildings. In March, 1893, the Committee of Twelve appealed to Governor Elias Carr in Raleigh, asking for his advice and assistance in helping the black residents keep their property.

We the citizens of James City have been there for thirty (30) years and all that we have accumulated within 30 years are in James City, and all we have are about to be taken from us (two thousand people more or less) we ask you are there any such law as this, to take a man's house and all the property from us. We admit that the land is not ours, but the houses and property on the land belongs to us. We are law abiding and have always been. It is hard to be dispossed [sic] [after] 30 years hard labor and toil. You will be pleased to favor us with your advice by return mail and oblige the committee of James City.[41]

Governor Carr responded to the committee by declaring that the courts had decided the case and that the residents of James City should abide by a Craven County sheriff's writ, obtained by Bryan, to dispossess them of the land. He vowed to use "the military power of the state" if they did not honor the sheriff's request. "It would be a thing unheard of in the history of the state," the governor warned, "that a plaintiff could not recover real property through the ordinary process of the laws, which the courts of the state have declared by solemn adjudication to be his."[42]

In an effort to terminate his dispute with the tenants, Bryan offered them a number of concessions. He proposed to reduce the rents and to lease the lots to them for three additional years. He excepted the waterfront lots, on which he reserved the right to terminate leases at any time. Those who would accept a three-year lease were given permission to move their houses (if they were known to have constructed them) at the end of the period, providing they had paid all of their rent. Bryan would allow all "old and infirm" people who lived alone to remain for three years rent free and would charge no rent for "churches, schools, and lodges." The congregations or trustees of these institutions could remove those buildings at the end of the lease period. In no instance would Bryan lease the land for longer than three years, and at the end of

---

[41] James City Committee of Twelve to Governor Elias Carr, March 15, 1893, Governors Letter Books, Elias Carr, 1893-1897, GLB 90, p. 31, State Archives, hereinafter cited as Governors Letter Books, Carr.

[42] Carr to James City Committee of Twelve, March 17, 1893, Governors Letter Books, Carr, GLB 90, pp. 30-31.

that period, he stated, he alone would decide if new agreements would be made.[43]

By the time Bryan had made this offer, the black settlement had divided into two factions. One group supported the position of the Committee of Twelve and its chairman, Paul Williams, that the inhabitants purchase the land from Bryan and settle for nothing less. Another, led by Robert R. Davis, wanted to accept Bryan's stated terms or at least to reach a mutually satisfactory agreement with him. Unwilling to remain divided, the residents united behind the Committee of Twelve and insisted that they be permitted to buy the James City tracts from Bryan.

Upon hearing of the blacks' rejection of his proposal, Bryan in exasperation announced:

The terms of settlement by me to you some time since having been rejected by the portion of your people represented by Paul Williams and others, and not having been complied with by that portion of the inhabitants represented by R. R. Davis and others, I hereby notify you that I hold myself no longer bound by them. I now consider the property in the hands of the law and await its action to place me in possession thereof.[44]

On April 19, 1893, Craven County Sheriff William B. Lane with deputies and wagons set out for James City to serve a writ of possession and to force the inhabitants off Bryan's property. Since the early days of Reconstruction the ringing of a church bell had been a warning signal to the people of James City that it was threatened by intruders from outside. The bell could be heard for long distances and was used to summon members of the village who were working in New Bern or in nearby sawmills or fields or who were fishing to return immediately and defend the community. Blacks in the settlement had rung the bell before Sheriff Lane arrived. According to the *New Berne Weekly Journal*, this resulted in "those in this city dropping their employment instantly and rushing over to join the crowd."[45] The sheriff immediately encountered resistance. "On my arrival," he reported, "I found all the buildings (there are about 500 in number) closed and locked and the entire population assembled in the Streets, and was plainly and emphatically told that . . . if we valued our lives we had better not attempt to break and enter any buildings."[46]

---

[43] *New Berne Weekly Journal,* April 13, 1893.
[44] *New Berne Weekly Journal,* April 13, 1893.
[45] *New Berne Weekly Journal,* April 27, 1893.
[46] William B. Lane to Elias Carr, April 19, 1893, Governors Letter Books, Carr, GLB 90, pp. 37-38.

Lane attempted unsuccessfully to persuade those who had assembled to obey the writ and vacate the premises. Hopelessly outnumbered, he and his deputies quickly returned to New Bern. He then tried to raise among the whites in the county a larger posse with which to enforce the court order but found few volunteers.[47]

Mayor Matt Manly of New Bern wrote to Governor Carr that the people in the town were alarmed by the presence of so many blacks hostile to white authority. He pointed out that many of the citizens feared a black insurrection spearheaded by the inhabitants of James City. "We have," he wrote, "to consider the protection of New Berne of a white population of 3000 people and 7000 negroes[;] what cause they will take in the event of trouble with James City we cannot tell. It is certain that some of the negroes will take part with their friends across the Trent." The mayor stressed that James City blacks were "one in sentiment and action" and would fight if a posse attempted to evict them. He asked the governor to provide Sheriff Lane with a detachment of militia if the latter requested it.[48]

Before making such a request from Governor Carr, Lane awaited the outcome of a conference between a contingent of black ministers of New Bern and residents of James City. The clergymen hoped to convince the village people to accept Bryan's last offer and avoid violence. But James City blacks once again rejected those terms. Upon hearing of the rejection, the sheriff wrote to Governor Carr: "I am sorry that I cannot report favorably on our troubles with the James City negroes. The clergy reported . . . that they would not hear or entertain any proposition, but to purchase the lands." He asked the governor to send 400 troops "to help me enforce the law." Lane estimated that there were 500 "able-bodied men" in the settlement, many of whom owned Colt and Winchester repeating rifles. Although a unit of naval reserves was then stationed in New Bern, he reported that they were primarily poorly trained "boys" who would be of little value in a heated fight.[49]

Upon receiving Lane's urgent message, Carr ordered State Adjutant General Francis H. Cameron to assemble the First Regiment of North Carolina militia and prepare to leave for New Bern. The companies that made up the regiment came from various counties, and on April 24 part of this force mustered in Raleigh. They were to travel by rail to New Bern and to join with the remainder of the regiment at Goldsboro. They departed the capital on that day amid a great deal of fanfare.

---

[47] Lane to Carr, April 19, 1893, Governors Letter Books, Carr, GLB 90, pp. 37-38.
[48] Matt Manly to Carr, April 19, 1893, Governors Letter Books, Carr, GLB 90, p. 39.
[49] William B. Lane to Carr, April 19, 20, 21, 1893, Governors Letter Books, Carr, GLB 90, pp. 37-40.

The troops moved down Fayetteville and Martin streets at 1 o'clock in their brilliant uniforms while hundreds of spectators massed on each side viewed them as they marched.

At least two hundred ladies as well as a great crowd of citizens were at the depot to see the soldier boys start. The train left on schedule with the troops aboard, and a throng of ladies and a great crowd waving their handkerchiefs and bidding the boys adieu.

Governor Carr, along with an entourage of government officials and newspaper reporters, accompanied the troops. The various companies, totaling about 375 men and equipped with "three heavy guns," arrived at New Bern late in the afternoon and set up camp on the fairgrounds. The Committee of Twelve immediately called on the governor in New Bern, and he agreed to meet with them in James City on the following day.[50]

Shortly before the meeting commenced, the militia officers and the press set out to dramatize the situation. The officers ordered their men to drill diligently and make a show of force. Reporters, using exaggerated prose, initiated hourly telegraphic accounts of events at James City. "The press association is here," wrote one correspondent. "The pen is mightier than the sword, but does not glitter as much."[51]

Governor Carr boarded a train and crossed the Trent to confront the black protestors. Accompanying him were a number of government officials, reporters, and a committee of eight black leaders who had joined the troop train at Goldsboro. The latter, including E. E. Smith, who had been a minister to Liberia in Grover Cleveland's first administration, were present to attempt to argue against the use of violence. Furnifold M. Simmons was also in attendance.

When the train arrived in James City, some of the village's inhabitants were assembled around a speaker's stand decorated with flowers. Some parents, fearing violence, had previously removed their children from the settlement. Isaac Long remembers that his mother took him to a relative's house outside of James City and returned to the village to attend a special church service held prior to Carr's arrival. Alexander Delemar's band struck up a martial air as Carr stepped from the train. After accepting the welcome of the blacks, the governor proposed that he hold a private conference with the James City Committee of Twelve. Trailed by his entourage of reporters and politicians, he and the James City committee adjourned to the community's Samaritan Lodge, where they met for an hour.[52]

---

[50] *News and Observer*, April 25, 1893.
[51] *News and Observer*, April 26, 1893.
[52] *New Berne Weekly Journal*, April 27, 1893.

During the meeting the black lawyers and Congressmen James E. O'Hara and George H. White, who were representing the residents of the village, urged them to accept the three-year lease with Bryan. Not to be outdone by these political rivals, Furnifold M. Simmons managed to interject some words to the James City committee. He "used his voice effectively in behalf of law and showed them how they were bringing themselves into ill repute and how all attempted evasions of the law— locking of doors and other subterfuges[—]were unavailing. . . ." The committee of blacks from Goldsboro likewise advised the community's representatives to accept Bryan's proposal and avoid bloodshed. Governor Carr declared that while he sympathized with the black residents, the courts had decided the case and he would have to uphold the law and put them off the land if they could not reach any agreement with Bryan.

The Committee of Twelve agreed to meet with Bryan and try to reach some mutual solution; and they promised to report the outcome of the meeting to Carr by 3 o'clock that afternoon. At the conclusion of the conference the governor mounted the speaker's stand, informed the waiting crowd what had just been decided, and also delivered some "words of extreme kindness coupled with firmness." Then at 11 o'clock he and the others who had arrived on the train boarded it again and went back to New Bern.

Because he had "had so much trouble with the James City people," James A. Bryan at first refused to renew his offer of three-year leases except to "the few who [earlier] had signified their willingness to make terms." But after a conference with the governor, Bryan agreed to grant leases according to his most recent proposal. He further stipulated that the tenants would be bound by the lease for the full three years and that there could be no subletting. The size of lots could not exceed 50 by 100 feet, and rents would be 50 cents to $1.00 per month. The Committee of Twelve agreed to these terms, and a potentially violent racial conflict was avoided.

The residents of James City signed leases with Bryan on April 26, 1893.[53] It is not certain how many, if any, left the community rather than accept Bryan as a landlord. Most of the residents apparently chose to remain as part of the community even if it meant they could not predict their future beyond the ensuing three years. Shortly after Bryan and his tenants reached an agreement, the governor returned to Raleigh and the militia withdrew from New Bern; the only casualty of the military movement was a colonel who suffered a fall from his horse during a drill and died a short time later.[54]

---

[53] New Berne Weekly Journal, April 27, 1893.
[54] News and Observer, April 28, 1893.

Having gained clear ownership of the James City property, Bryan set out to make it turn a profit. He began by advertising for rent to various lumber companies portions of the waterfront land not actually occupied by the blacks. By 1893 three companies had rented sites in the James City vicinity. These were the Blades Lumber Company, the New Berne Lumber Company ("Prettyman Mill"), and the S. H. Gray Manufacturing Company. The latter firm produced wooden plates, dishes, and bisulphate wood pulp. These companies held five-year leases at a cost of $95 per year.[55]

Nevertheless, Bryan still hoped to sell the property outright to a northern manufacturing firm or a large lumber company that would be willing to purchase thousands of acres and establish an industrial center. He considered James City well suited for the textile or lumber industry and emphasized the village's proximity to the Atlantic & North Carolina Railroad and to water transportation as an important reason why the property should be acquired for industrial purposes. Writing to a prospective buyer in November, 1895, Bryan extolled the virtues of the place:

I am not so anxious to part with the property James City . . . as I am to make of it a great manufacturing point.

It is upon the south bank of the Trent River immediately opposite this place & connected there with by the bridge of the Atlantic & North Carolina R.R. about 600 yards in length.

There are in the tract about 2500 acres with a water front of three or four miles.

The town of James City begins at the Southern terminus of the bridge & contains about 2500 inhabitants—a little beyond the town on the lines [?], are located the lumber plants, saw mills, dry kilns &c. The deep water is near the shore & there are sites—for a number of factories.

The Rail Road runs through the town & any vessel that can come in at Hatteras inlet can be within a few feet of the shore.

This is a fine cotton section . . . & timber of great [worth] & abundance is within easy reach by both rail and water. We have daily association with the country by Sail & several steamers . . . to northern ports. Our climate is good & our labor both black and white is cheap, abundant, efficient, and intelligent. We have no labor organizations & consequently no strikes or other disturbances incident thereto.

But the great advantage of this property is freedom from all Municipal taxation, & the growing development of the section. I see no reason why it should not become in the very near future the seat of a busy place of industry, & therefore

---

[55] *Sanborn Fire Insurance Map of New Bern, North Carolina, 1893* (New York: Sanborn Map Company, 1893), hereinafter cited as *Sanborn Insurance Map of New Bern,* with appropriate year. The industrial sites at James City are shown on the New Bern maps.

regard it as a most advantageous position for the profitable investment of capital. . . .[56]

Bryan hired a New York agent to promote his Craven County holdings among northern and foreign investors. He hired an agent, William Beard, who advertised the property and distributed printed circulars that described its advantages for economic development. Bryan informed Beard that he wanted the best price for his acreage. "As to James City," he wrote in December, 1896, ". . . I want Five hundred thousand dollars for it . . . as I have told you it will eventually be the business point of this section & I am in no hurry to sell it."[57]

James C. Delemar, James City contractor and grandson of bandleader Alexander Delemar, points out the deteriorated pilings that once supported a number of wharves on the banks of the Trent River near James City. The wharves were constructed by lumber companies that were established in the area during the late nineteenth and early twentieth centuries and which provided an important source of employment for James City residents. James Delemar's father was employed by one of these firms. Photograph (1980) by Walton Haywood; from the files of the Division of Archives and History.

But Bryan's hopes for establishing a large industrial center on the land never materialized, and he ultimately resorted to the less ambitious practice of renting lots on the James City waterfront to various sawmill and lumber companies. These companies built docks at James City on the shores of the Neuse and Trent rivers. There their schooners

[56] James A. Bryan to Andrew Dutcher[?], November 21, 1895, James A. Bryan Letter Book (No. 136), p. 134, Bryan Family Papers, Southern Historical Collection, hereinafter cited as Bryan Letter Book (No. 136).

[57] James A. Bryan to William Beard, December 3, 1896, Bryan Letter Book (No. 136), p. 268.

picked up cargoes of lumber that had been cut from nearby forests and processed at local mills. These vessels carried their cargoes northward to seaports, particularly Baltimore and Norfolk.

In 1898 the S. E. Sullivan Sawmill had also acquired a site in the James City area, and by 1904 the Munger and Bennet Saw and Planing Mill had located there. By 1908 Munger and Bennet, the Mills-Campbell Lumber Company, and the Carolina Pulp Company were operating in the vicinity of the village. The John L. Roper Lumber Company came about 1900 but was dismantled prior to 1908.[58]

At the end of the three-year period previously agreed upon, Bryan, having failed in his attempt to sell the James City tract, renewed the

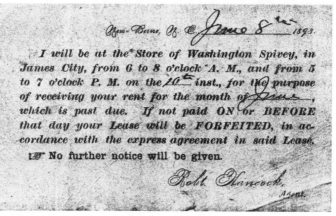

James A. Bryan, a wealthy white landowner of Craven County, obtained control of the property comprising James City in 1880. Bryan consistently refused to sell any of the property to local black residents and instead entered into lease agreements with individual tenants. He then appointed Robert Hancock as his agent to collect the rents. In this broadside Hancock announced his intention to *"be at the Store of Washington Spivey, in James City"* on June 10, 1893, for the purpose of collecting rent. Broadside supplied by James C. Delemar, James City.

leases of a majority of the village's black residents. According to Bryan, the people were "anxious" to renew their leases, and he felt it was "partly to my interest to make the leases."[59] Many of the tenants found work in the nearby saw- and lumber mills and in other skilled or unskilled trades. The largest number of blacks, however, continued to work as farm laborers.[60]

---

[58] *Sanborn Insurance Map of New Bern, 1898; 1900; 1904; 1908.*
[59] James A. Bryan to William Beard, May 18, 1896, Bryan Letter Book (No. 136), p. 233.
[60] Long interview, March 24, 1980; Twelfth Census, 1900, Craven County, Population Schedule, 107-127.

Bryan was more persistent in the collection of rents than had been the Evans family. He appointed Robert Hancock, "a bitter Republican partisan who held the office of collector of customs under [Benjamin] Harrison's administration," to collect the fees. In collecting the rents, Hancock usually went to Washington Spivey's store on the tenth day of each month, and the tenants went there to pay him. But not all of them could or would pay, and Hancock frequently threatened them with eviction. In 1896 Democratic editor Josephus Daniels suggested that Bryan's association with Hancock as well as his refusal to support the leasing of the state-owned Atlantic & North Carolina Railroad to private enterprise suggested that Bryan harbored Republican sympathies.[61] If Bryan possessed such sentiments, he had abandoned them by 1899 when he was elected to the state Senate as a Democrat.

During the closing years of the nineteenth century the people of James City continued to live much as they had since the Freedmen's Bureau departed the area. But afoot in the state and region at that time was a movement that would significantly alter the lives of blacks in James City and throughout the South: a political campaign built upon the notion of "white supremacy." The campaign was launched in 1898 by Furnifold M. Simmons, then chairman of the state Democratic Executive Committee, in an attempt to eliminate permanently the Negro from the political process and regain for the Democrats the control of state government that had been lost to the Republican-Populist fusion in the election of 1894.[62]

In Craven County the white supremacy campaign was implemented in large part as a consequence of the failure of the Democratic party to gain the black vote. The relationship between Furnifold M. Simmons and the inhabitants of James City illustrates this point. Simmons had won election to Congress in 1886 from North Carolina's Second Congressional District primarily as a result of a division of support within the ranks of the Republican party between two black candidates, James E. O'Hara and Israel B. Abbott. In the election of 1888, however, no Republican schism existed, and Simmons knew he must make a concerted effort to persuade blacks to support him in his bid for reelection to Congress in order for him to defeat Henry P. Cheatham, a black Republican candidate. To win the support of James City blacks, Sim-

---

61 *News and Observer*, November 21, 1896; broadside, notification for collection of rent in James City by agent Robert Hancock, June 8, 1893, in possession of James C. Delemar, James City.

62 Helen G. Edmonds, *The Negro and Fusion Politics in North Carolina, 1894-1901* (Chapel Hill: University of North Carolina Press, 1951), 136-154, hereinafter cited as Edmonds, *The Negro and Fusion Politics*.

mons obtained for a local black man the position of postmaster and secured for the town of New Bern congressional appropriations for a new federal highway project and construction of a federal building. These projects would provide employment for many of James City's residents. Despite Simmons's efforts to woo them politically, the people of James City, like blacks throughout the Second Congressional District, refused to vote for him and instead elected Cheatham to Congress in 1888. "I did not obtain a vote from James City," Simmons lamented, "not even that of the Negro postmaster." Simmons's experience in the election of 1888 apparently taught him that patronage and appeasement would not influence black voters and that other means would be necessary to ensure absolute political control of the state by whites. Unable to convince blacks to vote for him, Simmons came ultimately to embrace white supremacy and disfranchisement of Negroes as the only way Democrats could be elected in those sections of North Carolina in which whites constituted a minority of registered voters.[63] By 1898 Simmons and his party, having tasted defeat at the hands of the Republican and Populists, abandoned traditional political tactics and instead conducted a campaign based almost exclusively on the issue of race. Democrats set about to keep blacks from the polls through intimidation, manipulation of elections, and fraud. White-supremacy organizations such as the "Red Shirts," who were most active in the southeastern portion of the state, resorted to violence to prevent blacks from exercising their right to vote.

If intimidation by white supremacists occurred in Craven County in 1898, it failed to prevent James City blacks from voting in the election. Nevertheless, at the close of the contest the Democrats had regained political control of Craven County and the entire state government.[64]

A "logical result" of the 1898 campaign was the enactment of so-called Jim Crow laws in North Carolina.[65] These were statutes designed to legitimize a policy of racial segregation by requiring that separate public facilities be established for whites and blacks. The first such law, passed by the legislature in 1899, required railroad companies operating in the state to provide separate cars for white and black passengers. After the turn of the century North Carolina enacted legislation declaring that racial segregation be observed in neighborhoods, streetcars, and

---

[63] J. Fred Rippy (comp. and ed.), *F. M. Simmons, Statesman of the New South: Memoirs and Addresses* (Durham: Duke University Press, 1936), 16-18.

[64] Edmonds, *The Negro and Fusion Politics*, 148-151; Lefler and Newsome, *North Carolina*, 556-559; Craven County Election Records. See specifically Volumes C.R. 028.912.1 and 028.912.2.

[65] Edmonds, *The Negro and Fusion Politics*, 189.

other public facilities. One such law even specified that black and white public school students could not use the same textbooks. In actual practice, racial segregation transcended the stipulations prescribed by law and became an established social institution in the state.[66]

Residents of James City, like blacks throughout the state and region, were affected by the Jim Crow laws and the institutionalization of racial segregation. But because James City blacks were then part of a separate and exclusively black community, the impact of segregation may not have been as great for them as for other blacks who were more closely tied to white society.

Even more than that of 1898, the election of 1900 proved harsh for blacks. During this campaign white political terrorists such as the Red Shirts were probably more active than in 1898.[67] Craven County whites who wanted to end black suffrage and office-holding formed organizations known as "white supremacy clubs"; these groups were especially visible in Craven County just prior to the election. On July 31, 1900, the *New Bern Weekly Journal* reported that "The meeting in this city, yesterday, of the White Supremacy clubs of Craven County, was a notable one in point of attendance, and in the reports made of the white supremacy movement throughout the country. The white men of Craven County are serious in their determination for White Supremacy, and the meeting of the White Supremacy Clubs was a living witness to the fact." [68]

In an effort to remove blacks entirely as a political factor in the state, the legislature, controlled by Democrats, proposed an amendment to the state constitution that would disfranchise most Negroes in North Carolina. The suffrage amendment, as it was known, stipulated that all citizens who registered to vote must have paid a poll tax and be able to read and write any section of the constitution. Such a literacy test would have disfranchised illiterate whites as well as blacks, but an additional provision of the amendment stipulated that "no male person, who was, on January 1, 1867, or at any time prior thereto, entitled to vote under the laws of any State . . . , and no lineal descendant of any such person shall be denied the right to register and vote at any election in this State by reason of his failure to possess the educational qualifications herein prescribed: *Provided*, he shall have registered in accordance with the terms of this section prior to December 1, 1908." In effect this provision,

---

[66] C. Vann Woodward, *The Strange Career of Jim Crow* (New York: Oxford University Press, second revised edition, 1966), 97, 100, 102.

[67] Lefler and Newsome, *North Carolina*, 560-561; Edmonds, *The Negro and Fusion Politics*, 198-214.

[68] *New Bern Weekly Journal*, July 31, 1900.

known as the "Grandfather Clause," exempted illiterate whites from the strictures of the suffrage amendment but had no effect upon illiterate blacks who as former slaves possessed no right of suffrage before 1867. Other states in the South likewise resorted to this tactic to restore permanent Democratic rule.

In the election of 1900 intimidation at the hands of the Red Shirts and white supremacy clubs kept blacks away from the polls. Election fraud also discounted Negro votes.[69] The *New Bern Weekly Journal* reported that in Craven County "the interest on the part of the white people was intense, while the colored people took little interest."[70] The Democrats won the election and the suffrage amendment passed. County election records indicate that the residents of James City did not vote in the election.

The political power of James City blacks, like that of Negroes throughout the South, had been ended by intimidation and extralegal measures that nullified the rights and privileges granted by the Fourteenth and Fifteenth amendments. After 1901, when southern blacks no longer had the right to vote, the Republican party abandoned its efforts to advance black interests. It became instead the "lily-white" Republican party, whose very existence revolved around federal patronage.[71] For many years thereafter, neither political party in the South attempted to reinstate the right of suffrage among the black population. In James City the inhabitants would not vote again until after World War II.[72]

---

[69] Edmonds, *The Negro and Fusion Politics*, 200-203, 209-210; Lefler and Newsome, *North Carolina*, 559-562.

[70] *New Bern Weekly Journal*, August 3, 1900.

[71] Edmonds, *The Negro and Fusion Politics*, 209-214; Craven County Election Records. See specifically Volumes C.R. 028.912.1 and 028.912.2.

[72] Author's interview with James C. Delemar, James City, June 4, 1980 (notes on interview in possession of author), hereinafter cited as Delemar interview, June 4, 1980.

EPILOGUE: 1901-1980

Although the people of James City entered into rental agreements with James A. Bryan in 1893, they began simultaneously to seek other ways of purchasing their own land and improving their fortunes. In May, 1893, the committee of eight Goldsboro blacks who had helped persuade the James City inhabitants to accept Bryan's offer wrote to Governor Elias Carr asking his help in securing land for the tenants. The Reverend R. L. Reeves spoke for the Goldsboro committee:

> Communications from the people of James City to the committee of eight colored citizens of Goldsboro who visited there two weeks since in the interest of law and order inform us that they intend to act upon the advice given them by your excellency and others and carry out in good faith their agreement with their landlord. In the mean time however they have been looking around to find purchasable land near by. They inform us that they have succeeded in finding such land, which could be bought in sufficient quantities to settle each family now residing in James City. These unfortunate people seem to regard us as their friends as well as the friends of law and order; hence they seek our counsel in the matter of attempting to buy houses. What shall we advise them? How can we serve them? These are questions which impress themselves upon us with much force. We are ready to do whatever we can to aid them, and feeling that His Excellency has sympathy for the unfortunate people in question we beg most respectfully to ask His Excellency to suggest to us something touching a suitable reply to the communications above alluded to.[1]

Carr replied that he sympathized with the James City residents but stood behind his earlier advice to them. "I beg to say through you to the people of James City," he responded,

> that I have no reason to change the advice given them on the occasion of my recent visit i.e. having paid their rents for three years it will be prudent for them to make haste slowly in the matter of purchasing new houses. By depositing their earnings in a bank for the next three years some opportunity will arise during that time in all probability to invest it more satisfactorily than the purchase of lands now. Please accept my thanks for the assistance rendered me by you and your committee while in New Bern which I highly appreciate. The James City People have my sympathy and I would be glad to aid them whenever in my power to do so.[2]

Most of the residents of the black settlement were forced to follow Carr's advice and postpone the acquisition of permanent homes. But others were able to buy lots on the nearby land to which the Reverend

---

[1] R. L. Reeves to Elias Carr, May 10, 1893, Governors Letter Books, Carr, GLB 90, pp. 51-52.

[2] Carr to Reeves, May 12, 1893, Governors Letter Books, Carr, GLB 90, p. 52.

Reeves had referred in his letter to the governor. The site on which they sought tracts was just across Scott Creek, south of James City. It was owned by S. H. Gray, whose factory was located nearby. In 1884 Gray had acquired the property from a black man named Jesse Brooks.[3] Somehow Brooks had become relatively wealthy during Reconstruction and had purchased the approximately 195 acres south of Scott Creek. Who Brooks was or how he became prosperous is not certain, but according to local tradition he had been a slave overseer before the Civil War and had acquired enough money to make financial investments after the conflict ended. The 1880 census listed him as a farmer living near James City.[4]

On October 26, 1893, Ralph Gray, son of S. H. Gray, entered into an agreement with the James City Committee of Twelve to sell to residents of the village a portion of the land his father had acquired from Jesse Brooks in 1884. Gray laid out 100 lots on 24 acres of land to accommodate those people from James City who could buy them. He called this new community Graysville. In 1895 he sold his holdings to J. A. Meadows and Company but excepted the Graysville land on which the people from James City were residing. Meadows later laid out lots on this property and sold them to other citizens from James City; he called this new settlement Meadowsville.[5]

With the exception of those who settled on the 100 lots in Graysville, most residents of James City entered into new rental agreements with James A. Bryan in 1896. Those who remained as Bryan's tenants continued their efforts to obtain permanent possession of land. About 1900 a number of them bought tracts in Meadowsville and adjacent communities known as Brownsville and Leesville, which also had been formerly owned by Jesse Brooks. As the blacks settled on these lands, they once again came to regard themselves as a single community and called their settlement (composed of Graysville, Meadowsville, Brownsville, and Leesville) the "new" James City.[6]

---

[3] Jesse Brooks to S. H. Gray and Alexander S. Peirce [sic], January 10, 1884, Craven County Deeds, Book 87, pp. 590-591.

[4] Delemar interview, June 4, 1980.

[5] Ralph Gray and wife to the E. H. & J. A. Meadows Company, September 5, 1893, Craven County Deeds, Book 111, pp. 426-429; Ralph Gray and wife to the E. H. & J. A. Meadows Company, October 26, 1893, Craven County Deeds, Book 111, pp. 578-580; the E. H. & J. A. Meadows Company to Ralph Gray, October 26, 1893, Craven County Deeds, Book 112, pp. 141-145; Ralph Gray and wife to the E. H. & J. A. Meadows Company, August 13, 1895, Craven County Deeds, Book 116, pp. 293-295.

[6] "Map of Graywood Farm and Adjoining Sub-Divisions of Meadowsville, Graysville, Brownsville, Graywood Place, Mooresville, Leesville, compiled from Recent Surveys by B. M. Potter, C.E., May, 1925," in possession of James C. Delemar, James City; Delemar interview, June 4, 1980.

This abandoned wooden structure is one of the few remaining remnants of "old" James City. Photograph (1980) by Walton Haywood; from the files of the Division of Archives and History.

But not all the former residents of "old" James City purchased land in the immediate vicinity. Some, like bandmaster Alexander Delemar and merchant Albert Butler (who had served in the African Brigade during the Civil War), secured land in the newly created black village of Columbia. This property had been a part of Clermont plantation, which was owned by Henry R. Bryan (brother of James A. Bryan). About 1893 Henry Bryan began laying out lots and selling them to the people of James City and other blacks who could afford them.[7] Other former tenants of James A. Bryan ultimately departed the New Bern area, particularly during World War I when strong demand for wartime labor existed in Norfolk, Baltimore, Philadelphia, and other large cities.

Austin Brown, who was born in James City in 1898, remembers that during World War I some of the local men served in the army. They left from the New Bern train depot, where the Delemar band (in which Brown played trombone) gave them a musical send-off. "Some of them didn't come back," he recalls, and others like Sammy Randolph, who was gassed and nearly blinded, suffered from wounds the rest of their lives. "I hated the war ended when it did," reflects Brown, who was about to enlist. "I was tired of plowing and wanted to see something else."[8]

---

[7] Plat maps of town of Columbia, n.d. [recorded December 20, 1893], Craven County Deeds, Book 112, pp. 292-295.

[8] Author's interview with James C. Delemar, George Lee, and Austin Brown, James City, August 4, 1980 (notes on interview in possession of author), hereinafter cited as Delemar-Lee-Brown interview.

Around the turn of the century James City lost its distinction as an exclusively black community when a group of Irish laborers moved into an area on the perimeter of the old settlement. They were few in number and worked as farmhands or found jobs in the nearby mills. One black resident of the period recalls that the blacks and Irish worked and socialized together and that the white people of New Bern had little regard for the Irish because of their free association with blacks. At the present time a few whites live within the borders of James City.

The people who remained in "old" James City after 1900 continued to pay rent to Bryan until his death in 1923 and to his heirs after that time. The number of tenants, however, steadily declined as more of them migrated from the old village to "new" James City or departed for cities or other rural areas. Residents of the old and new settlements maintained a close rapport and frequently acted as one community. They continued to worship together in the same churches and to observe the same social events and celebrations. During the first two decades of the twentieth century the churches were moved to the more recently established village.[9]

In the 1920s the residents of both old and new James City joined with other blacks in the area who were members of the Eastern Missionary Baptist Association and founded the Atlantic and North Carolina Industrial Institute. They erected the school by raising half the necessary expenses and securing matching funds from the Julius Rosenwald Fund, a philanthropic foundation that specialized in financing construction of public schools for blacks throughout the South. The school offered both academic and vocational courses and was under the supervision of the State Department of Public Instruction. In 1948 the citizens of James City built a lunchroom for the facility with their own materials and labor. The institute served the black community until 1957, when the state built a new school. (The students of James City are now bused elsewhere for classes, and the 1957 building is used as a community center.)[10] Residents of both sections of James City in the 1920s recall that there were a number of small stores and businesses located in the vicinity and even a "red light district" called "Black Bottom" in the older village. Those employed in the mills worked nine hours a day and five and a half days a week.[11]

---

[9] Delemar interview, March 24, 1980; Long interview, March 24, 1980.

[10] Craven County Records of Incorporation, Office of the Register of Deeds, Craven County Courthouse, New Bern, Record Book C, pp. 133-135; Delemar interview, June 4, 1980; "They Wanted a Lunchroom; They Worked and Got It," *State*, XV (May 22, 1948), 8-9.

[11] Delemar-Lee-Brown interview.

A typical street scene in "new" James City. Photograph (1980) by Walton Haywood; from the files of the Division of Archives and History.

The Great Depression of the 1930s resulted in hard times for James City. Agricultural laborers suffered as a result of scarce employment and small wages. The saw- and lumber mills closed, and the workers were without an income. Many inhabitants left the area in search of work. Those in the original settlement were hard pressed to pay rents, and some who lived there remember the Craven County sheriff arriving to collect fees or enforce eviction notices.

The outbreak of World War II ended the Depression and brought significant changes to James City. More of its citizens departed the area to serve in the armed forces or to take jobs in cities and war industries. After the war more funds were available to purchase land outside of "old" James City, and by the 1960s that village had virtually vanished. The last resident, William Spivey (a descendant of Washington Spivey), left during the early 1970s. The land that comprised the old settlement is presently owned by the Bryan heirs. A portion of the property has recently been taken up by U.S. Highway 70, which bypasses New Bern.[12]

Since the triumph of white supremacy in 1900, race relations have continued to be strained in North Carolina and throughout the nation. But in the James City area little overt conflict or violence has occurred between blacks and whites. The Ku Klux Klan burned a cross in the community in the 1920s but declined to confront the blacks directly. "They knew better than to start anything here," recalls Isaac Long.

---

[12] Delemar interviews, March 24, June 4, 1980; Long interviews, March 24, June 4, 1980; Assets, Inc., to J. Troy Smith, Jr., Trustee, and others, September 25, 1969, Craven County Deeds, Book 760, pp. 224-233; J. Troy Smith, Jr., Trustee, and others to Assets, Inc., December 22, 1969, Craven County Deeds, Book 764, pp. 558-562.

Some blacks from the area were active in the civil rights movement of the 1950s and 1960s.

Civil rights legislation and judicial decisions rendered during those two decades led to improved conditions for black Americans, and the people of James City shared in the resulting benefits. Isaac Long, who was born in the settlement in 1886, notes with pride that four of his grandchildren are college graduates.

At the present time the community's voters, most of whom support the Democratic party, are part of a strong black political force in the county and state. The extent of their influence was demonstrated in 1976 when they successfully lobbied against a proposal to extend the runway of nearby Simmons-Nott Airport; such an extension would have claimed the cemetery in which many of their ancestors are buried.

The present population of James City is estimated to be 700. Those who live there own their homes and land or rent from other blacks. Most residents are employed in New Bern, at Cherry Point Marine Air Station, or in other nearby towns.[13]

---

[13] Delemar interview, March 24, 1980; Long interview, March 24, 1980; *Sun-Journal* (New Bern), August 31, 1976.

APPENDIX

TABLE 1

Number of Freedmen Residing in
Federally Occupied North Carolina
January, 1864, and January, 1865

January, 1864

In New Bern and vicinity	8,591
In Washington and vicinity	2,741
On Roanoke Island and vicinity	2,712
In Beaufort and vicinity	2,426
In Plymouth and vicinity	860
On Hatteras Banks	89
Total	17,419

January, 1865

In New Bern and vicinity	10,782
In Beaufort and vicinity	3,245
On Roanoke Island and vicinity	3,091
On Hatteras Banks	95
In Plymouth and vicinity	94
Total	17,307

SOURCE: James, *Annual Report of the Superintendent of Negro Affairs in North Carolina, 1864*, 11-12.

TABLE 2

Occupations and Annual Incomes of
Leading Blacks Residing in New Bern and Vicinity

January, 1865

Ned Huggins, tar and turpentine	$3,150
George Hargate, turpentine farmer	3,000
W. A. Ives, carpenter and grocer	2,400
E. H. Hill, "missionary and teacher"	2,000
George Gordon, turpentine	1,500
Benjamin Whitefield, grocery and eating house	1,500
Limber Lewis, staves, wood, shingles	1,500
George Physic, grocer	1,500
Danzey Heath, grocer and baker	1,500
Adam Hymen, turpentine	1,300
Samuel Collins, dry goods and groceries	1,200
William Long, lumberman	1,200
John Bryan, cotton farming	1,100
Hasty Chadwick, turpentine	1,000
Sylvester Mackay, undertaker	1,000
Charles Bryan, coster	1,000
John H. Heath, shoemaker	1,000
Hogan Canedy, cooper and tar maker	1,000

SOURCE: James, *Annual Report of the Superintendent of Negro Affairs in North Carolina, 1864*, 11-12.

TABLE 3

Average Annual Income for Blacks in Various Occupations
New Bern and Vicinity, January, 1865

Grocers	$678
Barbers	675
Carpenters	510
Blacksmiths	468
Turpentine farmers	446
Coopers	418
Masons	402

SOURCE: James, *Annual Report of the Superintendent of Negro Affairs in North Carolina, 1864*, 11-12.

TABLE 4

Number of Northern and Black Teachers in Union-Held North Carolina, January, 1865

American Missionary Association (white) 22
New England Freedmen's Aid Society (white) 20
National Freedmen's Relief Association (white) 20
National Freedmen's Relief Association (black)[1] 4
Independent 2
Total ....68[2]

[1] The names of these black teachers were Richard Boyle, James Keating, Martha Culling, and Robert Morrow.

[2] Of these 68 teachers, 56 were women and 12 were men.

SOURCE: James, *Annual Report of the Superintendent of Negro Affairs in North Carolina, 1864,* 11-12.

TABLE 5

Approximate Population of Trent River Settlement (James City) and Number Receiving Aid from the Freedmen's Bureau January, 1865-June, 1867[1]

Date	Approximate Population	Number Receiving Aid
January, 1865	2,789	1,226
October, 1865	3,000	663
December, 1865	2,500	697
January, 1866	2,500	692
July, 1866	2,500	No aid given
December, 1866	2,000	665
June, 1867	1,660	34

[1] Aid given by the Freedmen's Bureau consisted primarily of rations and occasionally clothing and medicine.

SOURCE: James, *Annual Report of the Superintendent of Negro Affairs in North Carolina, 1864,* 11-12. Miscellaneous Ration Reports, November-December, 1866, and Reports of Rations Issued and Related Records, 1865-1868, Freedmen's Bureau Records, RG 105.

TABLE 6

Occupations of James City Residents, 1880

Farm laborers	281	Ferrymen	2
Housekeepers	113	Lumbermen	2
Farmers	87	Work in tobacco factory	2
Shingle makers	30	Work in plate factory	2
Laundresses	29	Porters in stores	2
Cooks	23	Work on railroad	2
Seamstresses	12	Missionaries (white)	2
Watermen	11	Brick mason apprentice	
Domestic servants	8	(works with father)	1
Stevedores	7	Grocer and farmer	1
House carpenters	5	Barber	1
Peddlers	5	Blacksmith	1
Work with General Ransom	5	Cooper	1
Clerks to hucksters	4	Night watchman	1
Work at sawmill	4	Sailor	1
Nurses	4	Stationary engineer	1
Schoolteachers (black)	4	Cook on a vessel	1
Ministers	3	Huckster	1
Painters	3	Clerk in store	1
Grocers	3	Porter	1
Wood sawyers	3	Gardener	1
Shingle maker apprentices		Works in hotel	1
(work with father)	2	Errand boy (youth)	1
Brick masons	2	Beggar (paralyzed)	1
Washwomen	2	Works in cotton factory	1
Draymen	2	Laborer	1
Ministers and farmers	2	Works in oyster saloon	1
Fish dealers	2		

SOURCE: Tenth Census, 1880: Craven County, Population Schedule, 211-222.

INDEX

A

Abbott, Israel B.: congressional candidate, 88; leads James City strikers, 72; mentioned, 71

"Act to Outlaw Felons Who Flee from Justice, An": discussed, 39-40

African Brigade: departs New Bern for duty in South Carolina, 18; mounts raid into northeastern North Carolina, 18-19; organized in Department of North Carolina, 16; pictured, 19; training performance of, appraised, 17; volunteers for, pictured, 17

African Methodist Episcopal Zion church: founded in New Bern, 10

American Freedmen's Union Commission (New York): mentioned, 50

American Missionary Association: commissions Russell School, 48; furnishes teachers, 29, 38; mentioned, 34, 41

Andrew Methodist Episcopal Church (New Bern): joins African Methodist Episcopal Zion Conference, 10

Atlantic and North Carolina Industrial Institute: founded, 95

Avon plantation (Pitt County): mentioned, 37, 42

B

Baker, Blount: quoted, concerning Federal soldiers' resentment of former slaves, 12

Ball, B. A.: donates clock to James City church, 70-71

Beals, H. S.: quoted, concerning appearance of Trent River settlement, 43

Beard, William: agent, hired by James A. Bryan, 86

Beaufort: large center for black refugees, 5; site of freedmen's camp, 23

Billings, Harriet S.: operates freedmen's school, 38; praises Horace James, 41

"Black Bottom": "red light district," 95

Blades Lumber Company: rents site near James City, 85

Boston Educational Society: commissions Russell School, 48

Boyden, David: mentioned, 40; overseer at Yankee Hall plantation, 39

Bray, Nicholas: mentioned, 14

"Bray affair": discussed, 14

Briggs, William T.: quoted, concerning illness of Horace James, 34

Brooks, Isaac A.: manages Lyon Pasture plantation, 45-46

Brooks, Jesse: former owner of lands comprising Brownsville and Leesville, 93

Brooks, Preston S.: mentioned, 26

Brown, Austin: recollections of, concerning World War I, 94

Brownsville: new community near James City, 93

Bryan, Henry R.: owns land that later becomes village of Columbia, 94

Bryan, James A.: agrees to renew offer of three-year leases of James City property, 84; attempts to collect rents from James City residents, 77; attempts to evict James City residents, 77, 79; brief biographical sketch of, 76-77; declares selling price for James City landholdings, 86; elected to state Senate, 88; mentioned, 95; offers concessions to tenants of James City, 80-81; quoted, concerning virtues of James City as industrial site, 85-86; renews rental agreements with residents of James City, 93

Bryan, Mary S. (Mrs. James A.): acquires James City property, 76

Bryan v. *Spivey et al.*: discussed, 79

Bryant, Furney: James City freedman and soldier, 19-20; pictured, 20

Bureau of Refugees, Freedmen, and Abandoned Land. *See* Freedmen's Bureau

Burnside, Ambrose E.: appoints Vincent Colyer superintendent of the poor for Federally occupied North Carolina, 4; faces problem of caring for and employing former slaves, 4; leaves New Bern, 15; mentioned, 1; orders Vincent Colyer to employ fugitive blacks to assist in war effort, 6

Butler, Albert: acquires land in village of Columbia, 94

Butler, Benjamin F.: initiates limited use of blacks as soldiers, 16; mentioned, 1; orders African Brigade into northeastern North Carolina, 18

C

Cameron, Francis H.: ordered to assemble troops, 82

Carolina City: site of freedmen's camp, 23

Carolina Pulp Company: operates near James City, 87

Carpenter, Edward W.: Republican judge, 78

Carr, Elias: accompanies state militia to New Bern, 83-84; advises James City residents concerning acquisition of homes, 92; meets with black protestors in James City, 83-84; orders troops to assemble for departure for New Bern, 82; responds to appeal from James City Committee of Twelve, 80

Cheatham, Henry P.: defeats Furnifold M. Simmons in congressional race, 89; elected to Congress from Second Congressional District of North Carolina, 67; receives overwhelming support of James City blacks in election of 1888, 88-89

Cherry Point Marine Air Station: mentioned, 97

China Grove plantation: mentioned, 71

Churches: centers of social life in James City, 75. See also Religion

Civil rights movement: mentioned, 97

Clermont Bridge: connects New Bern and James City, 74

Clermont plantation: mentioned, 94

Colored Ladies Union Relief Association (New Bern): mentioned, 18

Columbia: black village near James City, 94

Colyer, Vincent: appointed superintendent of the poor for Federally occupied North Carolina, 4; establishes schools for contrabands and poor whites in New Bern, 9, 10; headquarters of, pictured, 16; induces General Burnside to establish hospital for blacks, 9; leaves New Bern, 15; mentioned, 21; ordered by General Burnside to employ fugitive blacks to assist in war effort, 6; protests actions of Provisional Governor Edward Stanly, 15; quoted, concerning arrival of runaways in New Bern, 5; quoted, concerning employment of former slaves as Union spies, 8-9; quoted, concerning Furney Bryant, 20; quoted, concerning religious faith of former slaves, 10; quoted, concerning willingness of former slaves to assist Union army, 7; reopens freedmen's schools in New Bern, 15; takes census of contrabands in New Bern and vicinity, 5

Committee of Twelve: agrees to meet with James A. Bryan, 84; agrees to terms affecting three-year leases of James City property, 84; appeals to Governor Elias Carr for assistance, 80; calls on Governor Elias Carr in New Bern, 83; enters into agreement concerning land, 93; mentioned, 76; unwilling to compromise with James A. Bryan on question of land ownership, 81

Confiscation Act (1862): mentioned, 4

Congressional Reconstruction: discussed, 52, 53

Conservative party: mentioned, 53

Constitution of 1868 (North Carolina): mentioned, 53

Contrabands: origin of term, 1. See also Freedmen

Core Creek: mentioned, 71

County Government System: enables legislature to control county government in North Carolina, 67

D

Daniels, Josephus: mentioned, 88

Davis, Georgie: assistant school principal, 69

Davis, Robert R.: James City leader, 81

Dawson, A. B.: planter, 71

Delemar, Alexander: acquires land in village of Columbia, 94; bandleader, 75-76, 83; pictured, 75

Delemar, James C.: pictured, 86

Derby, William P.: quoted, concerning liberated slaves in New Bern area, 1-2

Disfranchisement (of Negroes): resorted to, by North Carolina Democrats, 90-91

Dismal Swamp Canal: mentioned, 18

E

Eastern Missionary Baptist Association: mentioned, 95

Elizabeth City: mentioned, 2

Emancipation Proclamation: generally understood by North Carolina slaves, 15-16; mentioned, 4

Emmerton, James A.: quoted, concerning eagerness of freedmen to obtain an education, 10-11; quoted, concerning escaping slaves, 2; quoted, concerning slaves' uncertain future as freedmen, 3

Evans, Peter G.: mentioned, 24, 47

"Exodusters": term for black emigrants, 72

F

Farmers Association of James City: goals of, 63; resolutions of, 62, 63
Fifty-fifth Massachusetts Regiment: mentioned, 16
First North Carolina Regiment. *See* African Brigade
Fitz, Edward S.: dismissed from Freedmen's Bureau, 57; supervisor of James City, 56; tried for mismanagement of Trent River settlement, 57
Folly Island (South Carolina): mentioned, 18
Fort Pillow (Tennessee): battle at, mentioned, 17
Fort Totten: mentioned, 7
Fort Wagner (South Carolina): mentioned, 18
Fortress Monroe (Virginia): mentioned, 1, 28
Foster, John G.: mentioned, 15, 18; selects Horace James as superintendent of Negro affairs for Federally occupied North Carolina, 21
Fourteenth Amendment (to United States Constitution): ratified by state legislature, 53
Free blacks: reside in New Bern during Civil War, 13
Freedmen: arrival of, in New Bern, 5; assist Union army in war effort, 7; attacks upon, in New Bern area, 55; construct fortifications in North Carolina, 6-7; educational facilities for, established in New Bern, 10; employed as Union spies, 7-9; greet newly arriving Federal troops, 4; pictured, 7, 8; serve as soldiers in United States Army, 16-20
Freedmen's Advocate (New York): quoted, concerning freedmen's stores operated by Horace James, 32; quoted, concerning Mrs. Horace James, 34
Freedmen's Bureau: attempts by President Andrew Johnson to discredit, 56; continued by Congress for indefinite period, 58; established by Congress, 33; established by Horace James in various North Carolina locations, 23; evidence of benevolent activities of, at James City, 58; weakened by policies of Johnson administration, 58, 59
Freedmen's school: interior of, pictured, 30

G

Galloway, Abraham H.: leads New Bern convention of blacks, 51
Garfield, James A.: death of, mourned by James City residents, 66-67
Gillmore, Quincy Adams: mentioned, 18
Goldsboro: mentioned, 2, 83, 84, 92
Grandfather Clause: discussed, 90-91
Grant, Ulysses S.: supported by James City residents, 66
Gray, Ralph: agrees to sell property in new community of Graysville to James City blacks, 93
Gray, S. H.: acquires property from Jesse Brooks, 93
Graysville: new community near James City, 93
Great Depression: effects of, upon James City, 96
Greeley, Horace: presidential candidate, 66
Green, Joseph: dispatched as James City delegate to Raleigh convention, 52
Grimes, Hurley: death of, 71; leader in organizing Farmers Association of James City, 62; pictured, 63
Grimes, Lamb: foreman at Yankee Hall plantation, 39
Grimes, William: mentioned, 37, 40

H

Haines, Z. T.: quoted, concerning abuse of former slaves by Union soldiers, 12; quoted, concerning recruitment for African Brigade, 16, 17; quoted, concerning religious practices of former slaves, 10; quoted, concerning slaves' reception of Federal troops, 4
Hancock, Robert: appointed by James A. Bryan to collect rents at James City, 88
Harper, Francis W.: Craven County sheriff, 59
Harris, George: quoted, concerning his flight to freedom, 6
Herald (New York): attempts to discredit Trent River settlement, 56-57
"Holt, Reverend": mentioned, 67
Hood, James Walker: pastor of St. Peter's A.M.E. Zion Church, New Bern, 10

pictured, cover, 46; political activity in, 51-54, 67-68, 88-89, 91, 97; population of, 68, 97; sanitary conditions in, 57-58; school in, described, 69-70; sentiment in favor of disbandment of, 55; site of, restored to Peter G. Evans family by federal government, 50; social events in, 75-76

"James's Plantation School, North Carolina": pictured, 38

Jennings, Thomas J.: quoted, concerning resentment of former slaves by Union soldiers, 12

Jim Crow laws: enacted in North Carolina, 89-90

John L. Roper Lumber Company: operates near James City, 87

Johnson, Andrew: strongly opposed to Freedmen's Bureau, 36, 54, 56

Johnson, Joseph B.: overseer at Avon plantation, 39, 40

Jones, Mary E.: reports on degree of literacy at freedmen's school, 50; reports on patronizing view of northern missionary officials, 50

Jones A.M.E. Zion Chapel (James City): mentioned, 67, 71

Julius Rosenwald Fund: mentioned, 95

K

Keel, Alsbury: death of, 39; mentioned, 40

Kinston: mentioned, 2

Ku Klux Klan: becomes active in North Carolina, 53-54; mentioned, 96

L

Laidler, Stephen W.: accuses Edward S. Fitz of mistreating freedmen, 56, 57; accuses Freedmen's Bureau of mismanaging James City, 56

Lane, William B.: attempts unsuccessfully to enforce writ of possession, 81-82; asks governor to send troops to New Bern, 82

Leesville: new community near James City, 93

Lincoln, Abraham: appoints Edward Stanly provisional governor of Federally controlled North Carolina, 13-14; devotion of freedmen to, mentioned, 29; mentioned, 4, 26; reassures Vincent Colyer concerning freedmen's schools, 15

Lodge: encourages labor unions, 72

Logan, Frenise A.: quoted, concerning ostracism of Negroes who voted for Democrats, 67

Long, Isaac: mentioned, 97; pictured, 70; quoted, concerning Ku Klux Klan, 96; recalls events connected with Elias Carr's visit to James City, 83

Lumber mills: mentioned, 85, 86-87, 96

Lyon Pasture plantation: mentioned, 45-46, 58

M

McPherson, James M.: quoted, concerning definition of abolitionist, 26

Manly, Matt: mayor of New Bern, 82; quoted, concerning fears of insurrection by James City blacks, 82

Meadows, J. A.: sells lots in new settlement known as Meadowsville, 93

Meadowsville: new community near James City, 93

Means, James: appointed superintendent of the poor for Federally occupied North Carolina, 15; dies of yellow fever, 21

Means, Kate A.: operates freedmen's school, 38

Miles, Nelson A.: reports on breakup of freedmen's camps in North Carolina, 61

Mills-Campbell Lumber Company: operates near James City, 87

Moore, Stephen: mentioned, 59; ordered to investigate conditions at James City, 63; quoted, concerning desire of James City freedmen to own land, 60

Morehead, John M.: grandfather of Peter G. Evans heirs, 61

Morris, Mr.: hired as teacher in freedmen's school, 50

Morrow, Robert: black teacher in freedmen's school, 30-31

Mount Shiloh First Baptist Church (James City): mentioned, 51; pictured, 51

Munger and Bennet Saw and Planing Mill: locates near James City, 87

N

National Freedmen's Relief Association: establishes school for blacks in New Bern, 29-30

New Bern: blacksmith and wheelwright shop in, pictured, 13; described as a "Mecca of a thousand noble aspirations," 5; fish market in, pictured, 74; freedmen's schools established in, 29-30; large center for black refugees, 1, 5, 23; map of, 44; mentioned, 97; school in, pictured, 11

New Bern harbor: pictured, 5

New Berne Lumber Company: rents site near James City, 85

New England Freedmen's Aid Society: furnishes teachers for freedmen's schools, 29

"New" James City: mentioned, 93; street scene in, pictured, 96

Norfolk (Virginia): mentioned, 18

O

O'Hara, James E.: congressional candidate, 88; elected to Congress from Second Congressional District of North Carolina, 67; represents residents of James City in negotiations with Governor Elias Carr, 84

"Old" James City: mentioned, 95; wooden structure surviving from, pictured, 94

P

Pearson, Sarah M.: quoted, concerning hazards of conducting classes during wartime, 48-49; teacher in charge of Russell School, 48-49

Peck, John J.: mentioned, 24

Pettigrew, James J.: mentioned, 31

Pickett, George E.: mentioned, 24

Plymouth: site of freedmen's camp, 23

Political Reconstruction: initiated in coastal region of North Carolina by Lincoln administration, 13

"Prettyman Mill": term for New Berne Lumber Company, 85

R

Randolph, Sammy: wounded in World War I, 94

Reconstruction Acts (1867): divide South into military districts, 52

Reconstruction Convention: meets in Raleigh, 51-52

Red Church (New Bern): striking laborers meet at, 72

"Red Shirts": white-supremacy organization, 89, 90, 91

Reeves, R. L.: writes to Governor Elias Carr on behalf of black leaders of Goldsboro, 92

Religion: importance of, to former slaves, 9-10, 29. See also Churches

Republican party: changes policy, 91; formed in North Carolina, 52

Roanoke Island: freedmen's camp established there by Horace James, 23; large center for black refugees, 5; mentioned, 7

Rogers, Hattie: quoted, concerning slaves' flight to freedom, 2

Roundtree, Henry: quoted, concerning treatment of slaves, 3

Russell, Daniel L.: supported by James City blacks, 67

Russell School: established by northern philanthropic organizations, 48

S

St. Peter's African Methodist Episcopal Zion Church (New Bern): 10

Salter, James: said to have bought James City property, 77, 78

Sawmills. See Lumber mills

Seely, F. A.: mentioned, 39; testifies in military trial of Horace James, 41

S. H. Gray Manufacturing Company: rents site near James City, 85

Sharecrop system: effects of, on residents of James City, 61-62

Sherman, William T.: mentioned, 25

Simmons, Furnifold M.: acts as attorney for residents of James City, 78; attempts unsuccessfully to win political support of James City residents, 88-89; launches white-supremacy campaign, 88-89; participates in meeting between Governor Elias Carr and residents of James City, 83, 84

Simmons-Nott Airport (New Bern): mentioned, 97

Slavery: conditions of, in North Carolina, 3

Smallpox: epidemic of, in New Bern, 9

Smith, E. E.: black clergyman, argues against violence, 83

Spaight, Richard Dobbs: mentioned, 23

Spivey, Washington: elected to local political offices, 68; leads James City residents in court battle against James A. Bryan, 77; mentioned, 88

Spivey, William: last resident of "old" James City, 96

Stanly, Edward: appointed provisional governor of Federally controlled North Carolina, 13-14; his career, briefly

described, 14; his involvement in the "Bray affair," 14; mentioned, 23; orders Vincent Colyer to close evening schools in New Bern, 14; resigns as provisional governor of North Carolina, 15
Stanly, John: mentioned, 23
Staunton, Edwin M.: authorizes creation of brigade of black troops in Department of North Carolina, 16; selects O. O. Howard as commissioner of Freedmen's Bureau, 33
Steedman, John B.: appointed to investigate Freedmen's Bureau, 40; attempts to discredit Freedmen's Bureau, 56; pictured, 56
Stevens, Thaddeus: mentioned, 64
Strikes: staged by black laborers to protest low wages and high prices, 71-72
S. E. Sullivan Sawmill: acquires site near James City, 87
Sumner, Charles: mentioned, 15, 26

T

Tappan, Winthrop: business partner of Horace James, 37
Tarboro: mentioned, 2
Teachers: accomplishments of, in New Bern area freedmen's schools, 50
Thomas, Rachel: establishes school for freedmen at Trent River settlement, 50
Trent River: mentioned, 74
Trent River camp. See James City
Trent River settlement. See James City
Tucker, E. E.: addresses striking laborers, 72
Tucker, John S.: addresses striking laborers, 72
Twenty-fifth Massachusetts Regiment: members of, volunteer as teachers at freedmen's schools in New Bern, 10

U

"Union scouts" (spies): pictured, 9
United States Army: efforts to recruit black soldiers for, in New Bern, 16

W

Walker, Nancy: schoolteacher, 69
Washington (North Carolina): large center for black refugees, 5; mentioned, 2, 7; site of freedmen's camp, 23
White, George H.: elected to Congress from Second Congressional District of North Carolina, 67; represents residents of James City in negotiations with Governor Elias Carr, 84
White-supremacy campaign of 1898: discussed, 88-89
White-supremacy clubs: formed by Craven County whites prior to election of 1900, 90, 91
Whittlesey, Eliphalet: acquitted of charges brought in military trial, 41-42; advises freedmen of termination of aid from Freedmen's Bureau, 54; appointed assistant commissioner of Freedmen's Bureau for North Carolina, 33; appoints Horace James financial agent for Freedmen's Bureau in North Carolina, 33; business partner of Horace James, 37; establishes headquarters for Freedmen's Bureau in North Carolina, 33; mentioned, 44, 48; quoted, concerning civil rights of Negroes, 59; quoted, concerning laws on homicide, 39; regrets resignation of Horace James from Freedmen's Bureau, 36; reports on number of destitute freedmen, 54
Wiegel, W. W.: attempts to reduce population of James City, 58
Wilcox, Tom: quoted, concerning slaves' desire to control their own destiny, 3
Wild, Edward A.: authorized to organize brigade of black troops in Department of North Carolina, 16; pictured, 19
Williams, Paul: chairman of James City Committee of Twelve, 81
Willis, George: school principal, 69
Winston, George F.: his views on relations between Union troops and former slaves, 12; quoted, concerning freedmen's perception of Emancipation Proclamation, 15-16; quoted, concerning qualifications of Union soldiers to teach in freedmen's schools, 11; quoted, concerning services rendered Union troops by New Bern blacks, 12
World War I: mentioned, 94
World War II: effects of, on James City, 96

Y

Yankee Hall plantation (Pitt County): mentioned, 37, 42
York, Amos: mentioned, 67

109

THE BENNETT PLACE

By Arthur C. Menius

This report, prepared as an in-house research resource, documents the historical events connected with the Bennett Place, a simple wooden farmhouse in present-day Durham County, North Carolina, that was selected as the site for meetings held in April, 1865, between Union General William T. Sherman and Confederate General Joseph E. Johnston for the purpose of negotiating terms for the surrender of forces under Johnston's command. The agreement reached at the farmhouse by the two generals hastened the end of the Civil War. The report also traces the efforts of concerned citizens to preserve the Bennett Place site as a memorial park, to focus public attention on the historical significance of the property, and ultimately to construct on the site a facsimile of the original farmhouse and exterior kitchen.

James Bennitt[1] (ca. 1807-1878), a yeoman farmer, acquired a tract of land in northern Orange County (now Durham County) in 1846. There he erected a small wooden farmhouse, engaged in diversified agricultural pursuits, and supplemented his income with cobbling, tailoring, and other activities. By the 1850s Bennitt and his family had achieved a moderate level of prosperity. Accounts and records maintained by Bennitt present an unusually detailed portrait of a small antebellum North Carolina farm.

By early March, 1865, when Union forces under the command of General William T. Sherman entered North Carolina, both of Bennitt's sons and his son-in-law had died. Following the Battle of Bentonville (March 19-21, 1865), Confederate troops under the command of General Joseph E. Johnston could no longer offer serious resistance to Sherman, and Federal forces quickly captured Goldsboro and Raleigh. Over the objections of Confederate President Jefferson Davis, Johnston sued for peace. By chance Generals Sherman and Johnston agreed to meet for a conference at James Bennitt's farmhouse on April 17 and 18, 1865. Sherman, fearing a protracted period of guerrilla warfare and believing that he was carrying out the policies of recently assassinated President Abraham Lincoln, proposed to Johnston generous terms for restoring peace to the nation.

---

[1] James Bennitt consistently spelled his surname with an *i*. The use of the second *e* originated in references to his house in the letters of Civil War correspondents and reporters and was repeated in the works of historians of the era.

Post-assassination Washington was unwilling to accept the liberal terms set forth by Sherman and rejected the agreement while casting aspersions on Sherman's loyalty and character. A potentially tragic stalemale was averted when Sherman and Johnston held another meeting at the Bennitt farmhouse on April 26 and agreed to simple, acceptable conditions for terminating hostilities.

James Bennitt died in 1878, and his farmhouse passed through the hands of several owners before being destroyed by fire in 1921, leaving only a brick chimney. In 1923 a portion of the land on which the house had stood was acquired by the Bennett Place Memorial Commission, a public association formed for the purpose of maintaining the site as a memorial park. During this period preservation of the former Bennitt property became the personal project of Durham attorney and state legislator R. O. Everett, Sr., who labored for many years thereafter to keep public interest in the site alive. In 1958 funds from private sources became available to construct on the site a facsimile of the Bennitt farmhouse and kitchen. Two period wooden buildings whose general dimensions corresponded closely to the Bennitt structures were moved to the property and altered to conform to the appearance of the originals. In 1961 these structures and their surrounding grounds were designated as the Bennett Place State Historic Site. At present the Bennett Place is maintained and administered by the Historic Sites Section of the Division of Archives and History.

HISTORICAL AND ARCHITECTURAL DEVELOPMENT OF TARBORO, NORTH CAROLINA

By Catherine W. Bishir and Joe A. Mobley

This research report, based on primary and secondary sources as well as extensive architectural fieldwork and oral-history resources, treats the history and architectural development of the Edgecombe County town of Tarboro from its establishment in 1760 to the present. Tarboro is of particular interest in that its history encompasses a variety of periods of growth and is representative of important developments throughout the state. This study documents specific aspects of the town's history and utilizes examinations of specific persons, events, and buildings to exemplify larger trends.

Tarboro began as an inland river port and government center for the English colony of North Carolina. The town was also the home of many political leaders of the eighteenth-century colony and state. A key element from this era is the survival of the original town plan, notably the open common north and south of the traditional street grid—a rarely enduring example of eighteenth-century town planning.

Tarboro flourished during the antebellum years of cotton prosperity. It was the commercial center of a county acclaimed for its advanced farming techniques, and many of the successful local planters resided in or near the town. Surviving examples of antebellum suburban villas, with their uncommon styles of landscape gardening, are indicative of cultural activity associated with the small town.

In the post-Civil War period Tarboro produced a number of important black leaders who were politically active on a statewide basis. The town came to embrace industrialization in the late nineteenth century, and it continues to retain important aspects of the cotton and fertilizer industries so important to the revitalization of the economy of a traditionally rural state.

During the early twentieth century the community was a leader in efforts to modernize, with a municipal milk plant, improvements in sanitation, an early telephone company, and several regionally important businesses exemplifying the spirit of that era. In the mid-twentieth century Tarboro's growth resulted in the destruction of a number of significant architectural resources from its past, but recent work in preservation has succeeded in developing new approaches.

The research report, prepared as part of a National Register nomination, is an unusually thorough study of an important and little-studied North Carolina town.